THE
SYMBOL
DETECTIVE

THE
SYMBOL
DETECTIVE

HOW TO DECIPHER MYSTICAL MOTIFS
—AND KNOW WHERE TO FIND THEM

TONY ALLAN

DUNCAN BAIRD PUBLISHERS
LONDON

The Symbol Detective
Tony Allan

Distributed in the USA and Canada by
Sterling Publishing Co., Inc.
387 Park Avenue South
New York, NY 10016-8810

This edition first published in the UK and USA in 2008 by
Duncan Baird Publishers Ltd.
Sixth Floor, Castle House
75–76 Wells Street
London W1T 3QH

Managing Editor: Christopher Westhorp
Managing Designer: Daniel Sturges
Editor: James Hodgson
Picture Researcher: Susannah Stone

Library of Congress Cataloging-in-Publication Data available

ISBN-13: 978-1-84483-617-8   ISBN-10: 1-84483-617-7

1 3 5 7 9 10 8 6 4 2

Typeset in Gill Sans
Color reproduction by Colourscan, Singapore
Printed in China by SNP Leefung Printers Limited

For information about custom editions, special sales, premium and corporate purchases, please
contact Sterling Special Sales Department at 800-805-5489 or specialsales@sterlingpub.com.

Notes:
Abbreviations used throughout this book:
BCE Before the Common Era (the equivalent of BC)
CE Common Era (the equivalent of AD)

CONTENTS

INTRODUCTION

Symbols are a hidden language, working not by direct reference but rather by a subtle process of allusion. Understanding them properly sometimes requires background knowledge stretching across cultures and centuries, for they may draw on stories and traditions whose origins range back into the mists of time. Tracking them to their sources requires careful detective work, and this book sets out to serve as a guide.

Sometimes, of course, a symbol can be so familiar that the meaning is plain for all to see. There is nothing uncertain, for example, about the significance of the Stars and Stripes flag or the images on motorway signs or airport information panels. Yet behind these instantly recognizable images lies a hinterland of more mysterious signs and signals whose full purport is not always obvious, even when the general drift is acknowledged as a matter of convention.

These more obscure symbols are the subjects of this book, which sets out to untangle some of their unexpected connotations and connections. What links owls with wisdom, for example, or olive branches with peace? Why was a small animal often sent over a newly built bridge before any human would dare use it? As the world of myth, legend and folklore that many symbols reference recedes further into the past, they increasingly need explanation to spell out their secret meanings.

Most of the symbols in this book imply their message rather than stating it directly. Generally they tend to suggest interpretations, based on hints and associations, rather than insisting on them unambiguously. Sometimes the people who first used them had good reason for choosing clandestinity over clarity. For example, the early Christians who drew fish designs on the walls of the Roman catacombs faced brutal persecution if they openly avowed the beliefs that the image symbolized.

To tease out the associations of the world's better-known symbols, this book divides into two principal parts. The first addresses the different types of symbol, broken down by their sources, say in abstract patterns and shapes or in the natural world. It also covers some major fields of symbolism, such as light and fire, and time and death. Many of the individual emblems covered are cross-referenced in the book's second part, which examines the use of symbols in the world's religions and belief systems, traditionally the most widespread and prolific users of symbolic imagery to convey key elements of their ideology and doctrines. This is the section to consult to find out why ancient Egyptians viewed the humble dung beetle as a solar symbol, to learn about the Gnostic origins of the incantation "abracadabra", or to check out the Vel of Murugan and discover why it is worshipped in temples in southern India.

The book, then, is organized as a user's manual. Anyone seeking to understand the basic outward emblems of, say, Jainism or the Rosicrucian order can seek out the information in the latter part of the book. To learn more about the significance of the Rosy Cross that gave the latter movement its name, they can then turn to entries respectively on the Rose and the Cross in the earlier section, where they will find further material on the wider associations of each symbolic object.

This book is a wide-ranging introduction to an endlessly fascinating world of hidden meanings. It seeks to entertain and to inform, and in so doing to cast an often unexpected light on details of the world around us as we experience it from day to day.

PART ONE

TYPES OF SYMBOL

- -

Symbols divide between abstract and physical.
All language, for instance, falls in the first
category. Others, though, have a concrete
reality over and above the concept they stand
for – a flaming torch may be just that unless
the occasion is the Olympic Games, when it
represents the Olympic spirit. In this way many
objects take on secondary meanings that can
vary in different settings. This section of the
book examines some common groupings.

PATTERNS AND SHAPES

Basic building-blocks of meaning

Almost every shape known to humankind has some symbolic significance, from the dot (the still point of origin and regression) through the square (four-sided, solid, balanced) to the mystic circle, unbroken and suggestive of the infinite and the universal. The numbers are almost limitless: one scholar claims to have collected 60,000 signs and marks from all the world's cultures. Ways of organizing space, patterns and shapes can draw on subconscious mental responses to convey meaning. Thus, a forward-pointing triangle becomes an arrowhead suggesting direction and onward motion. Yet, purely abstract concepts can also be expressed – witness the mathematical symbol for infinity or the familiar Chinese *yin-yang* mark. Consequently, patterns and shapes have always figured strongly in religious imagery, and also in such fields as astrology and magic.

EYE OF
PROVIDENCE
Enclosed in
a triangle,
connoting the
Christian Trinity,
the all-seeing
eye features
in Mormon
and Masonic
imagery, as well
as appearing
on US dollar
bills and the US
Great Seal (see
page 148).

Circle

The circle always had cosmic significance. Early sky-gazers observed not only the Sun and the full Moon, but noted the rotation of the planets. These early astronomers visualized the universe itself as a series of flat discs or as a sphere. Having no beginning or end, the circle also came to stand for completeness, perfection and eternity. Then again, all points on its circumference are equidistant from its centre, suggesting equality and a lack of hierarchy, as in King Arthur's Round Table, as well as inclusion and protection (see box, opposite). All these varied qualities helped early on to lend the circle a mystical aura. Folklore had its fairy rings, Neolithic art its mysterious cup and ring markings. Stupas – Buddhist shrines – are circular in cross-section, and the faithful circumambulate them as an act of worship. Interlocking circles are a symbol of union, as in the Olympic logo.

Triangle

An equilateral triangle conveys the coming together of three equal parts, a quality that led to its use as a symbol of the Christian Trinity. Other religions too developed a tripartite concept of godhead, often featuring

three separate deities. The Hindu *trimurti* combined Brahma, Vishnu and Shiva, bringing together the figures of creator, preserver and destroyer, sometimes represented as a single being with three heads. Later Zoroastrian tradition also recognized three divinities as *ahuras*, gods worthy of worship, while modern Wiccans venerate a triple

---

THE HELM OF AWE

Incorporating crosses, a circle – or cosmic wheel – and forks, the Norse motif known as the "helm of awe", or *aejilshir*, also invoked qualities associated with the numbers three, four and eight. The *aejilshir* was mentioned in the Icelandic *Edda*s as a symbol that protected the wearer and induced fear in the viewer. In Germanic art the motif was depicted as an eight-pointed star. In both regions, warriors adorned themselves with the device as part of a cult of invincibility before going into battle, displaying it either on their helmets or their foreheads. In Wagner's *Ring* cycle, the magic helmet Tarnhelm was derived from the *aejilshir*. Norse myth related how this symbol belonged to Odin, and there was another tale explaining how Loki stole it from the treasure hoard guarded by the dragon Fafnir.

MALTESE CROSS
Formed of four arrowheads joined at their tips, this symbol was the emblem of the Knights Hospitallers, later known as the Knights of Malta.

SQUARE
Each of the intersecting woodpecker's heads on this Mississippian gorget represents a cosmic direction.

goddess, sometimes interpreted as incorporating in herself three aspects of womanhood: maiden, mother and crone. Reversed, the triangle recalls the pudenda, often serving as a female symbol.

In general, the triangle's religious symbolism emphasized stability and balance. Yet, by a visual pun, the shape could also resemble an arrowhead, suggesting movement. The Viking *valknut* or walknot, incorporating three linked triangles (see illustration, page 11), seems to have drawn on this imagery to denote Odin's power to release warriors' spirits. Upward- and downward-pointing triangles were the alchemical symbols for, respectively, fire and water.

Cross

Ubiquitous as a Christian symbol, the cross began life much earlier as a sign denoting quartets: the four winds, the phases of the Moon, the points of the compass. Cross shapes appear on megalithic monuments (the intersecting lines providing four points of direction). While Christianity drew on the cross as an instrument of torture and death, another tradition linked it to the World Tree or Tree of Life connecting Earth and Heaven. Crosses could also symbolize conjunction or coming together. Chinese symbolism saw five elements in a cross, counting the centre point as a position of power. Similarly, folk tradition around the world accorded magical significance to the crossroads, invariably a place of evil omen. In the Classical world crossroads were the haunts of Hecate, an underworld goddess who wandered at night accompanied by ghosts, demons and howling dogs.

Square

The symbol systems of India and China, two of humankind's most venerable cultures, both used the square as the sign for the Earth.

It symbolized permanence, balance, solidity and rationally organized space. Today, city planners with a taste for order often conceive new towns in terms of square blocks and right-angle junctions, emphasizing the rational over the accidental or natural in the communities they build. By a logical extension, squareness is also associated with moral rectitude in such phrases as "a square deal".

Cube

A square in three dimensions, the cube represents the same principles as the square to an even greater degree. Its six faces are identical; when they cease to be so through the addition of different numbers of dots, the cube becomes a die, a symbol of random chance. The cube also features as an emblem of centrality, notably in one of the world's most famously symbolic structures – the Kaaba in Mecca, focal point of the Muslim world.

Pentagram

The pentagram may have originally acquired its reputation from astronomy: seen from Earth, Venus appears to move around the zodiac in a pentangle shape every eight years. The connection with Venus dates back at least to Babylonian times, when the pentagram was associated with Ishtar, who manifested herself in the planet. Pythagoreans called the pentagram *hygieia*, the name also given to the goddess of health, and saw it as a symbol of mathematical perfection. Their followers identified the five points with the elements water, earth, air, fire and spirit. Cornelius Agrippa and other European

BIRDMAN
An image
from Easter
Island shows
a birdman
cradling an
egg. The figure
relates to an
annual contest
to fetch the
first seabird's
egg of the
year from
an offshore
islet. The
winner was
crowned as
Tangata manu
(Birdman).

occultists revived that connection in early Renaissance times, paving the way for the symbol in modern magick. While Christians saw it as a protection against Satan and the evil eye, Satanists adopted a version with two points facing up and a goat's head inscribed within as the Sigil of Baphomet, a powerful maleficent force. More recently Wiccans and some Neo-Pagans have chosen a more beneficent form, with a single point in the ascendant, as a common symbol.

Hexagram

Formed of two interlocking equilateral triangles, one pointing up and the other down, the hexagram is best known as the Jewish Star of

THE INFINITE

Early cultures had difficulty coming to terms with the notion of infinity; the Chinese for one tended to circumvent the problem by using "10,000" or some other very large number in its place. The man who devised the symbol (∞) now used to denote the concept was a 17th-century English mathematician named John Wallis. Some authorities speculate that he derived it from the letter w (omega), the last in the Greek alphabet; in the biblical Book of Revelation, God says

$$A \Omega$$

"I am Alpha and Omega" (letters, centre) to indicate the totality of His creation. Others, more prosaically, have suggested that it was a matter of convenience: in the days when typesetting was done by hand, the character could easily be composed by placing an "8" on its side. A third possibility is suggested by the word "lemniscate" that is sometimes used for the symbol; *lemniscus* was Latin for "ribbon", and the figure suggests an endless band.

David, but it also appears decoratively in Muslim, Hindu and Buddhist contexts. Occultists used it as a talisman and to conjure spirits.

Egg

An obvious symbol of gestation and birth, an egg featured in many creation myths in the form of the Cosmic or World Egg. Eggs can also suggest rebirth, as in the Orphic mystery religion or the Christian habit of giving Easter eggs at the season of Christ's resurrection.

Wheel

As an image of perpetual motion, the wheel has widely different associations in different cultural contexts. The Romans linked it with Fortuna, the blindfolded goddess of fate, creating the image of the ever-turning Wheel of Fortune. Buddhists saw in it the Wheel of Destiny, rolling through the eternal cycle of birth, death and rebirth. Another tradition viewed it as an instrument of punishment: in Greek myth Ixion was condemned by Jove for lusting after Hera to spend eternity turning on a wheel of fire, and in Christian tradition St Catherine of Alexandria narrowly avoided a similar fate, subsequently lending her name to the familiar "Catherine wheel" firework.

Spiral

Spiral motifs appear around the world as a decorative feature. They are particularly associated with Celtic art, famously appearing on the entrance slab of the Newgrange burial complex in Ireland. They also show up in Polynesian designs, especially tattoos (see page 21).

THE HUMAN BODY

Images of the individual's potential

By a natural process of association, parts of the human body came to symbolize the functions most commonly linked with them. So an open mouth could stand for speech or for hunger, an eye for sight and, by extension, inner vision. Other connotations were more mysterious, such as the longstanding association of long hair with strength as reflected in the Sikh refusal to trim hair or beard or the biblical story of Samson. The body as a whole could carry a significance of its own. Leonardo da Vinci's famous sketch of Vitruvian Man encased within a square and a circle came to represent not just the Quattrocento obsession with proportion but also the sense of possibility contained within the concept of Renaissance Man itself. In other contexts, nakedness could imply either of the extremes of carnality or radical innocence.

PROPORTION Leonardo da Vinci drew the original Vitruvian Man symbol, seeking to illustrate a suggestion by the Roman architect Vitruvius that perfect human proportions corresponded to unchanging geometric laws.

Nudity

A symbol of primeval innocence in the Garden of Eden story, nakedness was subsequently adopted by sects like the Adamites and Dukhobors seeking to regain that state. Wiccans who perform their rituals skyclad are generally in quest of a closer communion with nature. The sense of "natural" or "unadorned" also underlies such phrases as "the naked eye" or "the naked truth". Yet, through its power to shock, nakedness can also be a form of power. The Roman author Pliny the Elder reported that a woman could drive away storms by uncovering herself, and in southern India farmers used to stand naked on drainage dykes and beat drums to stop the rain.

Head

A symbol for the rational mind, as in phrases such as "to keep (or lose) one's head", the head could also stand as a microcosm for the individual as a whole. Headhunters decapitated enemies to capture their vital essence.

Hair

When the Sikh Khalsa brotherhood vow not to cut off their hair or beard, they are making a statement about strength and masculinity. Yet long hair can equally well be symbolic of rebellion and freedom from convention, as it was for the "hippies" in the 1960s. In

THE POT-BELLIED GOD

A pot belly was seen in many historic cultures as a sign of good living. This was nowhere more true than in the figure of Hotei, the most popular of Japan's Seven Gods of Good Fortune. Hotei was in fact a Japanese version of a character venerated across much of East Asia, by Buddhists and Taoists as well as by followers of the Shinto religion. He seems to have originated in India as a monk who attained enlightenment for his good deeds – specifically, catching venomous snakes to stop them biting passers-by. In China he is known as

Budai and is often called the Laughing Buddha. Everywhere he is associated with plenty and contentment – traits symbolized by his protruding belly. A folk tradition persists that rubbing the stomach of a statue of the god brings good luck.

TRISKELION From the Greek for "three-legged" – as in the three-legged tables crafted by Hephaestos and mentioned in the *Iliad* – this leg motif is a regional symbol in Sicily, Brittany and the Isle of Man. It also exists in a spiral variant which has solar associations (see pages 150–151).

contrast, a shaved head is in several religions a sign of humility and renunciation of worldliness. When enforced by others, as on criminals or women collaborators in occupied Europe at the end of World War II, it becomes rather a mark of humiliation. Tearing one's hair was a traditional mark of mourning in the Middle East; scalping, like headhunting, was a way of removing an enemy's potency.

Eye

One of the most ancient ocular symbols was the Eye of Horus (see opposite) from ancient Egypt. Originally the all-seeing Eye of Ra, the sun god, the image was transferred to the falcon god Horus

HAND

Endlessly useful and multi-functional, the hand – together with speech – is probably the evolutionary adaptation that does most to distinguish humankind from the quadrupeds. Unsurprisingly, then, it generally serves as an image of power. A raised fist can be a symbol of brute force, as in the Nazi salute. An outstretched palm generally signifies interdiction, unless there is an eye inscribed in it, in which case it becomes the *hamsa* warding off the Evil Eye (see page 126). In contrast, a hand raised in blessing suggests the transfer of spiritual energy, for example in the Christian tradition of laying on hands. Some similar hand signals can have very different meanings: two fingers raised with the palm turned out constitutes Sir Winston Churchill's famous "V for victory", but with knuckles foremost the digits form a gesture of bitter abuse.

as he rose in popularity up the Egyptian pantheon. A sign of divine omniscience and protection, it was used in mummification rites to promote rebirth under the god's supportive aegis.

The Third Eye of later traditions was an organ of spiritual perception, that denoted special insight. For Muslims it represented clairvoyance and knowledge of the future, for Buddhists powers of meditation and a deep understanding of *dharma* and the four noble truths. For Hindus it

was the brow *chakra* (energy point), the eye of knowledge whose possession was indicated by a mark on the forehead of yogis and sages.

Yet eyes were not always beneficent. In North Africa and the Near East people feared the Evil Eye, representing the gaze of jealousy and malice, and took elaborate precautions to avert its invidious influence (see box, opposite).

Nose

Symbolizing the sense of smell just as the eye represented vision, the nose was also for peoples around the world a dangerous orifice through which the soul might takes its leave or evil spirits could enter. In ancient times corpses of Chinese noblemen had the noses plugged with jade.

Beard

In the ancient Middle East, beards were symbols of authority and dignity. Egypt's rare female pharaohs were sometimes portrayed

SMILEY FACE
The smiley-face icon was first popularized in the 1970s as a means of selling novelty items. Modern-day texting has led to a rise in similar-looking emoticons.

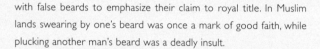

with false beards to emphasize their claim to royal title. In Muslim lands swearing by one's beard was once a mark of good faith, while plucking another man's beard was a deadly insult.

Breast

As with a woman's womb, represented by a swollen stomach, breasts were an obvious emblem of fecundity, most notably in statues of 100-breasted Artemis, the Earth Mother figure of ancient Ephesus. In Classical myth, milk from the breast of the goddess Hera was said to have formed the Milky Way, when she was suckling the infant Herakles and he pulled on the nipple too hard. Roman legend told of the women of defeated cities exposing their breasts to the conquerors as a plea for compassion and mercy.

Feet

Bare feet have long been a sign of poverty and humility. In the Middle Ages, the excommunicated Holy Roman Emperor Henry IV is said to have gone to Canossa barefoot in 1077 to beg forgiveness of Pope Gregory VII at the height of the Investiture Contest. Jesus similarly displayed humbleness by washing the feet of his disciples. In a very different spirit, defeated warriors might cast themselves at the feet of the victors, seeking mercy. In many traditions footprints had magical significance; some African peoples would even sweep the ground behind them lest the ground they trod on might be used by enemies for hostile magic. A foot-shaped indentation in a rock on the summit of Samanala, or Adam's Peak, a sacred mountain on Sri Lanka, has been variously interpreted by Hindus as the footprint of Shiva, by Buddhists the Buddha's, and by Christians and Muslims as that of Adam the first man.

HAIR
Long hair was prized by Native American warriors and, at times, ancient Greeks, such as Alexander (above).

Heart

Ubiquitous on Valentine cards in the West as a symbol of sentimental love, the heart also plays a part in Christian iconography as the sacred heart of Jesus (representing Christ's redeeming love), as shown in a vision to a 17th-century French nun, Sister Margaret Marie Alacoque. A flaming heart is a symbol of charity.

Another tradition associates the heart with courage – British sailors were traditionally said to have "hearts of oak" – or with innermost truth, as in the phrases "at heart" or "to take to heart". In similar vein, the French scientist and philosopher Blaise Pascal wrote in his *Pensées* that: "The heart has its reasons of which reason knows nothing."

More sinisterly, the Aztec belief that the Sun needed human blood to sustain it led their priests to rip out the hearts of an estimated 20,000 sacrificial victims annually, offering them as tokens to the gods.

TATTOOS

The decoration of human skin is an ancient practice. The "Iceman", from about 3300BCE, found in the Alps in 1991, had 57 separate tattoos. The corpse of a Scythian chief that was unearthed in the Altai mountains of southern Russia in the 1920s was covered with elaborate designs of beasts. The New Zealand Maori and other Oceanian peoples have a long tradition of body art, using the marks as signs of social status. The *moko* spiral facial tattoos of the Maori were fertility symbols, linked to the unfolding of fern fronds. Tattoos generally were seen as enhancements, advertising the courage of warriors or the beauty of maidens. They are still used today to display messages about an individual's identity.

COSMIC ELEMENTS

Signs in the sky

The sky and the elemental forces of nature lay so far outside most early peoples' frame of reference that they were instinctively assigned to the realm of the gods and spirits. So lightning was a weapon hurled from the hand of Zeus or Thor, thunder the rumble of a divine chariot careering through the heavens. Sun and Moon and stars were all visible emblems of godhead. In symbolic terms all the celestial features, from the planets and comets to rainbows and the wind, always retained something of the atavistic power they had before

MISSISSIPPIAN SPIDER GORGET

Celebrated by the Navajo as the deity who gave them the gift of weaving, Spider Woman is but one manifestation in the Americas – from the Mississippians of Cahokia to the Moche of Peru – of a popular reverence for this silk-producing arachnid. The spider and its web, seemingly so fragile yet so strong, made the creature a popular talisman for those seeking protection from the destructive power of the elements.

The mound culture of the American southeast identified the spider with the Sun and often used it as a decorative motif. Native American Mississippian myth claimed that the spider brought fire to humankind and this connection was evoked in Hopewell culture shell gorgets (ca.100BCE–500CE) with a rayed design – and sometimes a cross, for four cosmic directions – to replicate the Sun's rays and the flames of a fire (left).

modern science successfully explained them. Stars remained guiding lights or images of unattainable yearning, the rain the divine life-force – even, as some Gnostics believed, the semen of angels.

Sun

The Sun's primacy in the heavens inevitably made it a symbol of power, whether divine or terrestrial. Many religions gave the sun god

pride of place – examples include the Babylonian Shamash, the Persian Mithra and the late Roman cult of Sol Invicta. The first monotheistic cult was that of the *aten* or solar disk in ancient Egypt. In times of the divine right of kings, obvious parallels were also drawn between the sun's splendour and that of earthly monarchs. "Heaven cannot support two suns, nor Earth two masters", Alexander the Great is said to have exclaimed to emissaries of the Persian emperor Darius, making the comparison explicit. Few people took the solar connection more seriously than the Inca of Peru, who traced their ruler's descent to the Sun and ritually celebrated the link in daily ceremonies. In Europe, France had its own Sun King, Louis XIV, as recently as the 17th century.

Moon

Seen in ancient times as the Sun's celestial consort, the Moon tended to be viewed as female, the Queen of the Heavens – a link reinforced

by the coincidence that the duration of the female menstrual cycle approximates to a lunar month. The unblemished splendour of the full moon, at least as seen with the naked eye, led Buddhists to view it as a

HEPTAGRAM
The seven-pointed star was a symbol in the Kabbalah, and later used by the cult Ordo Templi Orientis. In Christianity it symbolized the seven days of creation and was used popularly to ward off evil. In the modern USA the emblem forms part of the police badge of the Navajo nation.

symbol of perfection, while its somewhat chilly purity also led to an association with chastity – Rome's moon goddess, for example, was the virginal huntress Diana. A similar line of thought made the Moon an emblem of unattainability.

The Moon has also always been emblematic of transience because of the endlessly repeated lunar cycle, from new to full and back. One phase that attracted particular attention was the crescent, which alchemists used to symbolize the metal silver (gold was represented by the Sun). In more recent times the crescent has been identified with Islam, though only through a distant historical accident – Muslims acquired it from the Ottomans, who had inherited it from Christian Constantinople, whose emblem it had been since Classical times.

Thunder

Thunder and lightning were hugely important to early cultures, which generally interpreted them as signs of divine wrath. Symbolically they were associated with superhuman powers, along with the thunderbolts supposedly hurled by the gods in the course of storms. The Hebrew God spoke to Moses in thunder when he gave him the Ten Commandments; Roman Jupiter was portrayed holding thunderbolts in his right hand, while the missiles were also the favoured weapon of the Norse god Thor. To Buddhists, the pronged thunderbolt, or *vajra* (right), is an emblem of the indestructibility of the final state of reality, known as *sunyata*.

Star

Star-watching is an ancient activity, along with the conviction that what happens in the heavens affects lives on Earth. In fact, most attention was always paid to the moving bodies – Sun and Moon along with the five planets known to the early world (Mercury, Venus, Mars, Jupiter and Saturn). While many cultures personified the five as gods – today they still bear the names of the associated Roman divinities – other peoples linked them with the souls of the dead. Algonquian peoples of North America referred to the stars as "grandfathers", and some early cultures claimed the Milky Way marked the path to Heaven.

Comet

Like other dramatic celestial phenomena, comets were traditionally seen as ominous, foretelling great events. Halley's Comet appeared in the Bayeux Tapestry as a portent of the Norman Conquest of Britain, while many scholars have suggested that the Star of Bethlehem might actually have been a comet. Early peoples tended to conceptualize comets in animal form as serpents or dragons.

Clouds

Most fundamentally, clouds were linked with rain and hence agricultural fertility. Yet in lands that had enough rainfall, they became symbols of sadness. Their serene position in the sky connected them to Heaven; the Pueblo people of southwestern USA, for instance, associated the Shiwanna or Cloud People with the spirits of the dead. Yet they also represented unreality; people still talk of an individual having his "head in the clouds" or dismiss dreamers as "living in Cloud-Cuckoo-Land".

NATURAL FEATURES

A geography of the mind

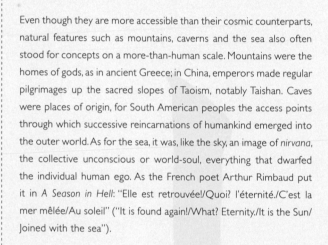

WAVES
The *seigaiha*
is a traditional
Japanese
pattern of
stacked waves
redolent of the
rippling sea.

Even though they are more accessible than their cosmic counterparts, natural features such as mountains, caverns and the sea also often stood for concepts on a more-than-human scale. Mountains were the homes of gods, as in ancient Greece; in China, emperors made regular pilgrimages up the sacred slopes of Taoism, notably Taishan. Caves were places of origin, for South American peoples the access points through which successive reincarnations of humankind emerged into the outer world. As for the sea, it was, like the sky, an image of *nirvana*, the collective unconscious or world-soul, everything that dwarfed the individual human ego. As the French poet Arthur Rimbaud put it in *A Season in Hell*: "Elle est retrouvée!/Quoi? l'éternité./C'est la mer mêlée/Au soleil" ("It is found again!/What? Eternity./It is the Sun/Joined with the sea").

Sea

The source of life in many creation myths, the sea was also long a symbol of eternity – the destination of all souls, just as all rivers run into the sea. Yet the embracing ocean waters were also home to storms and monsters – an image of the unconscious mind. Seemingly endless and unchanging yet also unpredictable and violent, the sea contained multitudinous contradictions, an emblem of primeval Chaos yet ultimately a place of rest.

Islands

From time immemorial people projected images of the happiness they sought somewhere beyond the horizon onto islands. Classical geographers spoke of the Fortunate Islands located in the Western Ocean, perhaps picking up the idea from Celtic legends of the Islands of the Blessed. St Brendan set off in search of them in the 6th century CE; accounts of his voyage seem quickly to have been confounded with the myth of Tir-na-Nog, the Land of Youth where sickness and ageing were unknown. Curiously, the Chinese had similar stories, in their case located in the east. The First Emperor, Shi Huangdi, sent an expedition in search of Penglai, the Island of the Immortals, in the 3rd century BCE, hoping to find the Elixir of Life; none of the hundreds of young men and women dispatched on the ships was ever seen again.

SACRED MOUNTAINS

Distant, ancient and remote, mountain peaks were seen by many early cultures as the home of the gods. The Greeks had Mt. Olympus; Moses went up Sinai to receive the Ten Commandments. Hindu cosmology made Mt. Meru the centre of the universe and the dwelling-place of Brahma and other deities. The closely allied Sumeru occupied a similar position in Buddhist thought.

In China the first land was thought to have been a mountain, surrounded by a vast ocean, and peaks are venerated by both Chinese Taoists and Buddhists, who identify a group of five and one of four sacred mountains respectively. The Chinese word for pilgrimage is a contraction of "respecting a holy mountain". This calligraphic symbol (above) represents the word "immortal" and it includes the Chinese characters for man (left) and mountain (right).

STRUCTURES

Towers of strength and stairways to Heaven

ZIGGURAT
The stepped
temples of
Mesopotamia
were, like the
pyramids of
Egypt, artificial
mountains,
designed to
raise the eye
and the mind
toward the
numinous
heavens.

A farming people, the ancient Chinese had a symbolic ideogram for "home" – a pig under a roof. Among structures themselves, however, the ones carrying the richest associative meanings tended to be those built for non-practical purposes: obelisks, labyrinths, pyramids, stupas. Such edifices were in many cases conceived as concrete expressions of abstract ideas – as stylized representations of the Cosmos, for instance, or as pointers directing the eyes heavenward. By a process of reinforcement, they themselves sometimes came to stand for the

LABYRINTHS

Myth records that the original Labyrinth was built in ancient Crete to house the Minotaur, half man, half bull and cannibalistic in its appetites. Taking its name from the *labrys* or double-headed axe that was emblematic of the Minoan civilization, it may actually reflect later Greek memories of the island's bull cult, honoured in the dangerous sport of bull-leaping. Later the word came to be applied to any complicated maze.

The adjective "labyrinthine", denoting endless complexity, suggests why labyrinths have come to be seen as symbols of the unconscious mind; the journey through them becomes analogous to the psychoanalytical quest for self-discovery. The idea of an inner, spiritual journey explains why ground-pavement labyrinths exist in some medieval Gothic cathedrals, such as Amiens, Chartres and Siena – and more recently in Grace Cathedral, San Francisco.

idea they were built to embody – stupas as visual mementoes of Buddhist enlightenment, ziggurats (opposite) as stairways to Heaven.

Tower

With their strong walls and high-rise design, towers were at once protective and aspirational. In fairy-tales of immured maidens, they essentially preserved chastity. In his poem *The Tower*, W.B. Yeats chose the image to symbolize the sage's lonely quest for wisdom. By reaching too close to Heaven, the Tower of Babel

became a symbol of human presumption. The Zoroastrian towers of silence where Parsees put out their dead to be consumed by birds of prey sought to separate the world of the dead from that of the living, preventing the defilement of the one by the other.

Pyramid

The pyramids of Egypt were funerary monuments that sought to immortalize the memory of the pharaohs responsible for building them – a task they have largely accomplished. They took the form of man-mountains, artificial hills rising toward the sky. The upward-pointing shape had significance in view of the belief that the pharaoh's spirit was reunited after death with the sun god, his heavenly equivalent. In their massive bulk they represented a defiant response to the inevitability of death at the same time as seeking to expedite the soul's passage beyond mortality.

Pillar

Ever since Freud, obelisks, pillars and columns have been viewed generically as phallic symbols, yet each also has specific implications.

PAGODA
Representing
the sacred
mountain,
a pagoda is
a form of
tiered tower,
traditionally
built with an
odd number
of floors and
often octagonal
in ground plan.

Obelisks – four-sided columns with pyramidal tops – were placed in pairs outside the portals of ancient Egyptian temples, partly to signify the importance of the edifices but also to serve a solar purpose – their gilded tips caught and reflected the Sun's rays. Pillars held up buildings and were emblems of strength; when Samson sought to assert his might against the Philistines, he did so by bringing down the temple pillars. Of the three, commemorative columns were perhaps the most obviously phallic in their intent. Built to honour great men (rarely women), they soared skyward as unambiguous celebrations of masculine pride.

Walled garden

The word "paradise" originally denoted the walled parks and pleasure-grounds of the Persian kings, and most ideas of an earthly paradise have since had a garden setting. The biblical Garden of Eden symbolized the primal innocence of the natural world, yet gardens as we know them are artificial constructs, symbolizing a happy cooperation between man and nature. Early Renaissance paintings made walled gardens the setting in which the rituals of courtly love were played out, perhaps recalling Eastern traditions of the sensual Perfumed Garden. Yet in the Christian tradition the image could also symbolize chastity: "A garden enclosed is my sister, my spouse," claimed the Song of Solomon, and painters often showed the Virgin Mary herself receiving the Annunciation in a walled garden.

Bridge

Bridges link what would otherwise remain apart, their connecting role emphasized in phrases such as "building bridges" or "bridge over troubled waters". So it seems strange that in folk tradition they

tended to be viewed with fear. People claimed that those who parted on a bridge would never meet again, and that the Devil would claim the soul of the first person to cross a new bridge (a small animal was usually sent over to allay the threat). Perhaps such fears hid memories of the bridges that in ancient religious tradition led to the Afterlife: the Muslim Al-Sirat, narrow as a sword's edge, or the Persian Chinvat, wide only as the deceased's own thoughts and deeds had been generous.

Triumphal arch

Roman emperors erected triumphal arches to celebrate their military successes, and the legions marched through them in victory parades. The form may have echoed ancient folk beliefs about the curative power of natural arches, particularly of brambles, which were thought to snag evil spirits and pathogenic agents when sick people passed beneath them. In similar fashion, passage through a triumphal arch may have separated the soldiers from the stain of bloodshed, not to mention the vengeful spirits of the men they had killed.

Stupa

Dome-shaped structures containing relics of the Buddha or of Buddhist holy men, stupas evolved from simple burial mounds into womb-like spaces sheltering precious souvenirs of sainthood and eventually into pagodas (opposite). A central mast rising from the top evoked memories of the bodhi tree under which Gautama himself found enlightenment.

TREES AND SHRUBS
Images of growth and fruition

CEDAR OF LEBANON
Prominent on the flag of Lebanon, the cedar is ancient and durable – immortal and incorruptible. Cedar resin was used by the Egyptians for mummification, and its rot-proof timber built Noah's ark, King Solomon's temple and the Ark of the Covenant.

Trees are among the biggest and most enduring of all living things, so from a human standpoint they naturally became symbols of strength and stability. Britain's sailors had hearts of oak, graveyard yews stood for perpetual remembrance. Norse myth spoke of the World Tree Yggdrasil, an ash that served as the axis of the universe. Yet trees in the plural could be threatening: South American shamans showed their hardihood by venturing out alone into the tropical jungle, while only intrepid knights were prepared to brave the Forest Perilous.

Tree of Life

A symbol known to cultures worldwide, the Tree of Life typically represented the continuity and fecundity of the natural world. Yet the actual species depicted varied widely – Babylonian and Assyrian artwork usually showed a date palm, a vital source of human sustenance at the time, while Chinese myth honoured the peach tree as the source of the fruit of immortality. Phrygian legends favoured the almond tree, while the ancient Celts revered the alder. The Mayans generally visualized the trunk supporting the world as that of a ceiba tree. Naturally enough, each civilization adopted a species essential to its own survival to express a universal truth.

Fig

Another sacred tree, the fig was venerated in Islamic lands because the Prophet Muhammad was recorded to have sworn by it. The tree also had a special place in Buddhism since Gautama Buddha found enlightenment under the bodhi tree, a Sacred fig (*Ficus religiosa*).

In Hinduism figs symbolized fecundity, being associated with the procreative powers of Vishnu and Shiva – a link perhaps suggested by the young fig's phallic shape and milky juice.

Almond

The almond tree traditionally had male progenitive associations, perhaps because of the semen-like juice exuded from its fruits. The Phrygian god Attis, worshipped in orgiastic rites across the Classical world, was supposedly born of an almond seed. Ancient tradition maintained that a virgin who fell asleep beneath an almond tree risked waking up pregnant. And in the Old Testament, Aaron's rod

OAK: FIRST AMONG TREES

The most widely venerated tree of all, the oak was, according to the ancient Greeks, also the first to be created. It played a central part at the oracle of Dodona in Epirus, where priests interpreted prophetic messages whispered to them by a sacred grove of trees. The oak was also holy to the Celtic Druids, who held their gatherings among oaks, and associated acorns (now usually symbols of patience and hard work) with hidden truth. Northern tradition maintained that oaks were the trees most likely to be struck by lightning, and Scandinavians associated them with Thor, god of thunder. The durability of oakwood was also legendary, causing the tree to be associated from early times with strength and fortitude, hence the use of oak-leaf clusters in martial awards for valour.

PLUM BLOSSOM Known in China as one, with pine and bamboo, of the "three friends of winter", plum is an emblem of resilience and marital happiness.

miraculously put forth ripe almonds overnight as a sign that his tribe of Levi was the fittest to provide priests for the Israelite people.

Pine

Strength and toughness have made the pine pre-eminent in China as a symbol of longevity. In Mesopotamia, the male generative force of the hero-god Marduk was symbolized by the phallic-shaped pine cone.

Olive

Olive wreaths symbolized victory when placed on the brows of winners at the ancient Olympic Games. Yet a more enduring association was with peace, perhaps because the olive tree and its fruit represented the sustenance and prosperity threatened by war. Romans used an olive branch as the emblem of the *Pax Romana*, and delegates from rebellious provinces bore one with them as an indication of submission. In the Christian tradition, the olive branch borne by a dove back to Noah's ark served as a peace pledge that God would send no more all-consuming floods.

Laurel

Whereas victors in the ancient Olympics wore crowns of olives, winners at the Pythian Games were awarded laurel wreaths (see page 89), hence the phrase "to look to one's laurels", meaning to protect one's competitive edge. Laurel was also viewed as a protective plant, warding off evil or (in the physical world) lightning – Emperor Tiberius always wore a crown of laurel during storms. In China the laurel was associated with longevity, ceding precedence only to the peach as the plant of immortality.

Holly

Holly's link with Christmas perpetuates the role it played in earlier midwinter festivals such as the Roman Saturnalia, when its green leaves and bright red berries symbolized hope in times of darkness. Christians adapted the symbolism to equate the redness with Christ's blood, given to redeem the souls of man to the eternal life suggested by the shrub's evergreen leaves.

Date palm

A masculine symbol in the Middle East, where it served as the Tree of Life for the Arab peoples, the date palm was associated in China with female fecundity. Romans carried palm branches in triumphal processions and accorded them as symbols of victory to successful gladiators, a habit commemorated in the phrase "to win the palm". Something of the symbolism of the conquering hero carried over into the behaviour of the crowd that strewed palm fronds before Jesus at the time of his entry into Jerusalem, as recorded in John's gospel. Thereafter the plants entered Christian tradition as the emblem of pilgrims to the Holy Land, known as "palmers" from their custom of bringing a frond back with them to decorate their local church.

Hawthorn

The white flowers of the early-blooming hawthorn were traditionally associated with girls in the springtime of their youth. Athenian maidens attending weddings wore crowns of hawthorn flowers, and the marriage torch itself was made of hawthorn wood. In the Victorian language of flowers, hawthorn stood for "Good Hope".

FLOWERS AND PLANTS

Flora's bouquet

FLEUR-DE-LYS
This heraldic
form of the
iris was the
emblem of the
kings of France
for more than
500 years.

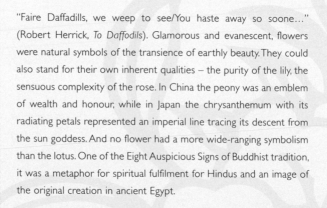

"Faire Daffadills, we weep to see/You haste away so soone…" (Robert Herrick, *To Daffodils*). Glamorous and evanescent, flowers were natural symbols of the transience of earthly beauty. They could also stand for their own inherent qualities – the purity of the lily, the sensuous complexity of the rose. In China the peony was an emblem of wealth and honour, while in Japan the chrysanthemum with its radiating petals represented an imperial line tracing its descent from the sun goddess. And no flower had a more wide-ranging symbolism than the lotus. One of the Eight Auspicious Signs of Buddhist tradition, it was a metaphor for spiritual fulfilment for Hindus and an image of the original creation in ancient Egypt.

Rose

ROSE
The white
rose was the
emblem of the
House of York
in England's
medieval Wars
of the Roses.

The cynosure of beauty in the Western tradition, roses were also indelibly associated with love in all its forms. The flowers were strewn through Aphrodite's temples in Classical times, and they turn up on innumerable Valentine cards to this day. Yet they also took on a mystical significance for the medieval authors of *The Romance of the Rose*, which portrayed the quest for love in spiritual terms, and the Christian Church identified them with the Virgin Mary and many female saints. While the red rose in particular signified passion, the blooms were also associated with the pains of love, as in the phrase "No rose without a thorn". The pleasure-loving Sybarites of Classical times slept in the original beds of roses, literally stuffed with the petals, and a story tells of a man tossing restlessly all night because a single one was crumpled. Yet even though most rose imagery was positive, a blown rose symbolized the transience of beauty, and Romans scattered the flowers on loved ones' graves.

Chrysanthemum

Japan's imperial flower is the spreading yellow chrysanthemum, widely seen as a symbol of order and perfection. The plant also became associated with longevity, possibly because it blooms late in the year. Yet white chrysanthemums are flowers of mourning in both Japan and China, commonly seen at funerals and on graves.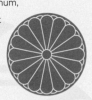

Iris

The iris was associated with the Virgin Mary, its sword-shaped leaves suggesting the pain of her grief at Christ's crucifixion. It also provided the inspiration for the fleur-de-lys (literally but inaccurately "flower of the lily"), a stylized image of an iris flower that became the symbol of the French monarchy from the 12th century on. The royal flag once featured an entire field of fleurs-de-lys, pruned down to just three by Charles V in the 14th century in honour of the Christian Trinity.

Lotus

Much of what the rose stood for in the Western lands was represented in the East by the lotus. The name is in fact now applied  to a number of different flowers, from the Common bird's-foot trefoil (Lotus corniculatus) to several varieties of water lilies. The most symbolically important species, the Indian or Sacred lotus, also grows on water but is now assigned a family of its own, the Nelumbonaceae. Like the rose, much of its symbolism had deep sexual roots, deriving from an unspoken resemblance between the unfurling blossoms and the human female sexual organs. So the flower came to play a central part in Hindu creation myths, which describe a single, giant lotus blossom emerging from the navel of Vishnu, bearing within it the creator god Brahma. Known as Padma, the name also of an associated goddess, the plant came to symbolize fruitfulness and creative power. And, again like the rose, it also served as a love token; Indian art is full of representations of Krishna presenting the flower to his lover, Rama.

THE BLOOD-RED POPPY

In Britain and other Commonwealth countries, the poppy has become indelibly associated with the dead of World War I, serving as the flower of remembrance for those who lost their lives in the conflict. Poppies grew freely on the killing fields of Flanders, thriving on the chopped-up soil, and the scarlet colour of the flowers naturally suggested a link with the blood shed around them. The association with death was not new; some early Christian authorities had suggested that the plant initially sprang from Christ's blood on the cross. An even stronger link was with sleep, suggested by the soporific effects of the opiates derived from *Papaver somniferum*, the Opium poppy.

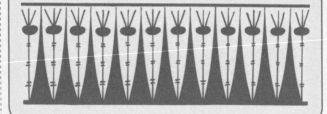

A separate tradition related to the lotus tree, a shrub of uncertain species mentioned in Greek mythology. It was the fruit of this latter plant that Homer's Lotus-eaters consumed, leading them to forget friends and duties and devote themselves to idleness and pleasure.

Peony

The peony takes its name from Paean, the surgeon of the gods in Homer but in other Classical authors a cognomen for Apollo in his capacity as a healer. Appropriately, the plant was long considered to have medicinal uses; in Japan, for instance, the roots were used to prepare anti-convulsants. It was also viewed as a protective plant in a more general sense – superstitious Europeans wore its seeds in necklaces as charms against epilepsy, cramps and the powers of darkness. Mostly, though, the flower has always been associated with showy beauty, being particularly admired in the Far East. In Japan it is still popular in bridal bouquets, while China has recently been considering adopting it as the national flower.

Lily

The immaculately white lily is a widely recognized symbol of innocence and purity that is perfect of its kind – to "paint the lily" is to foolishly seek to better what needs no improvement. Also linked to chastity, the flower became an emblem of the Virgin Mary, frequently appearing in Renaissance paintings of the Annunciation, often clutched in the hand of the Archangel Gabriel himself. Unsurprisingly, lilies later became favoured plants for church decoration. The flower can also symbolize innocence before the law; in parts of Europe a tradition arose that lilies would spring from the graves of wrongly executed felons.

Anemone

With a name from the Greek for "of the wind", the anemone's short-lived bloom was particularly associated with transience. The plant also linked with the death of Adonis in Classical myth, supposedly springing up from the nectar dropped by Venus on the bloodied ground where her loved one was fatally gored by a boar.

Amaranth

"The amaranth flower is the symbol of immortality," the Church father Clement of Alexandria recorded. The very word meant "that does not wither" in Greek, and Aesop in a fable contrasted the long-lasting blossom with the short-lived rose. The plant's reputation comes from its deep-red flowers – one of the best-known varieties, *Amaranthus caudatus*, is commonly known as Love-lies-bleeding – which retain their hue long after other surrounding blooms have faded.

Acanthus

Popular across the Classical Mediterranean world as an architectural and decorative motif (below, in an ornamental scroll), the acanthus shrub was identified with triumph over difficulties. In Christian iconography its thorns represented pain and punishment.

Thistle

The thistle's defensive prickles led to its adoption as the emblem of Scotland, first recorded in the 15th-century reign of James III. Its hardiness and tenacity caused it to be regarded in the East as a symbol of long life.

Ivy

Clinging and evergreen, ivy became a symbol of fidelity, and for Christians it also connoted eternal life. The ancient Greeks made it sacred to Bacchus, perhaps because of a folk belief that its poisonous berries slowed the onset of drunkenness.

Mistletoe

The complex symbolism of mistletoe draws on the plant's inherent botanical contradictions. A parasitical evergreen, it flourishes even when the host tree supporting it is seemingly dead. Although venomous, its branches and berries contain medicinal substances that once led it to be known as "all-heal"; even today, mistletoe lectins are used in Europe for cancer treatment. The spear that killed the beloved god Balder in Norse mythology was made of mistletoe wood, as was the golden bough that the Roman hero Aeneas carried as a protective talisman on his journey into the Underworld. Cursed and venerated in almost equal measure, Shakespeare's "baleful mistletoe" was held sacred by the Druids as an emblem of potency and fertility – an association that still lingers in Christmas traditions of kissing under the mistletoe bough.

FRUITS

Gifts of nature's bounty

APPLE
Indelibly associated with biblical Eden, the apple was an object of desire in Greek myth. The fleet-footed Atalanta agreed to marry any man who could outrun her. One suitor distracted her by throwing apples in her path, thus winning both the race and the girl.

As the most useful of plants, sustaining people physically as well as spiritually, fruit generally conveyed a positive message. In China the Tree of Immortality was a peach, and it bore fruit once every 3,000 years. The succulent pomegranate was naturally sacred to love goddesses, the intoxicating grape to divine trouble-makers like Dionysos. Yet the apple, wholesome enough to keep doctors at bay, could also serve as the Apple of Discord offered by Paris to Aphrodite, Hera and Athene.

Apple

Apples bear the scent of Paradise about them. Even though the fruit that Eve tasted in the Garden of Eden is never specified in the biblical text, the Celtic otherworld of Avalon meant "isle of apples", while in North America an apple tree was the central focus of the Iroquois heaven. The connection with health was also long-established: an Arabian Nights tale told of Prince Ahmed's apple that cured all ills, while the Norse gods started to age uncontrollably when Iduna, guardian of the golden apples of perpetual youth, was lured from her post by the malicious Loki.

Pomegranate

The luscious flesh and multiple seeds of the pomegranate early linked the fruit to fecundity. Chinese women made offerings of pomegranates to Guan Yin, the goddess of mercy, when praying for children, while in Turkey brides

would throw a pomegranate to the ground then count the seeds to find how many children they would bear.

Grape

Vines and the grapes that grow on them have generally served as an emblem of plenty. Like the "land flowing with milk and honey", the vineyard became a symbol of the biblical Israel, while in the New Testament St John's Gospel recorded Jesus as proclaiming, "I am the true vine, and my Father is the husbandman".

Orange

Evergreen and fructiferous throughout the year, the orange is a potent, international symbol of fecundity. Oranges were cultivated in China long before they reached the West, and the fruit is still associated there with luck and long life. In the 19th century, orange blossom became a conventional bridal decoration in Britain, symbolizing both the hope of fertility and the purity implied by the white blossom.

Peach

As the Chinese fruit of eternal life, the peach was associated with the Eight Immortals of Taoist legend. Gifts of porcelain bearing peach designs carried an unspoken wish that the recipient might enjoy long life and prosperity. Another association was with fertility – young brides were once commonly referred to as "peaches".

LAND CREATURES

Beasts of the fields and forests

LION
RAMPANT
Unusual for a
carnivorous
quadruped, the
standing lion
rampant forms
part of many
European coats
of arms and a
variant is part
of the royal flag
of Scotland,
introduced by
King William I
(1165–1214),
one of many
rulers to view
themselves as
"lion-hearted".

Human beings have lived near animals long enough to have formed firm, often contradictory, views of their characters and temperaments. Much of the symbolism of mammals springs from these perceived traits, ranging from the courage and strength of the lion, king of the beasts, to the legendary greed of the pig. Powerful individuals even sought to take on some of the characteristics for themselves. In animist religions, for example, it was common for shamans to don pelts as a way of assuming the attributes of the beasts they imitated. In similar vein, ancient Mexico's Olmec rulers traced their lineage to were-jaguars, half-animal figures that laid claim to some of the strength and ferocity of the top predators of the Mesoamerican jungle.

Bear

Bears have inspired as much fear as lions and tigers, but their almost human appearance, especially when raised on two legs, has made the relationship with people much closer. Along with the Ainu of Japan, several North American peoples traced their ancestry from bears, and folktales told of bears mating with women and fathering human children. Although a bear with a sore head became a comic symbol of irritability, the creatures could also be protective. Yet the main thrust of bear symbolism remained geared to brute force: Norse berserkers wore bear skins to go into battle, and the West's favoured Cold War image of Russian military power was of an angry bear.

Tiger

"Tyger, tyger, burning bright/In the forests of the night …" (William Blake, *The Tyger*). Another top predator, the tiger was less reputed for generosity of spirit than for its grace and power. In its haunts in southern Asia, where it served as the mount of the Hindu  warrior goddess Durga, there were many stories of shapeshifters taking on tiger form. In Korean folk medicine tiger bones ground into wine were supposedly fortifying in the literal sense.

Lion

Legendary for its strength and courage, the lion was a natural emblem of royalty from the earliest times. The Great Sphinx at Giza combined a lion's body with the head of the Pharaoh Khafre, while the lion-headed Sekhmet was a divine protectress of ancient Egypt's rulers. Assyrian kings celebrated their own power in magnificent bas-relief sculptures of themselves on lion-hunts. The analogy with power survived into modern times, as the lions in Trafalgar Square, symbolizing British imperial might, still attest. Yet for all its ferocity the lion could be generous to those who helped it, the story of Androcles being probably the best known of many folktales attesting to leonine gratitude.

Wolf

The big, bad wolf of fairytale is firmly fixed in the collective imagination as symbol of rapacity and greed. In Norse myth the Fenrir wolf swallowed the sun in the climactic battle of Ragnarok, German submarines in World War II roamed in wolf-packs, and

BOAR
The reverse of the boar's nobility was its brute ferocity: Shakespeare styled Richard III – who used the animal as a heraldic emblem – "the wretched, bloody and usurping boar".

werewolves famously brought out the beast in man (only rarely woman). For more positive lupine images one has to look either to dubious sources like the Turkish ultra-nationalists who have made the fascistic Grey Wolves heroes of their cause, or more promisingly to she-wolves like the one that nurtured Romulus and Remus, fierce warriors but also the legendary fathers of Rome.

Boar

Strength and resolution were the traditional qualities represented by boars, which featured strongly in myth from the Celtic to the Classical worlds, both of which had tales of epic boar-hunts. In Hindu

LORDS OF THE GLEN

Associated in popular culture today with Bambi-style innocence, deer in the past had a more assertive symbolic presence. To judge from cave paintings, stags played an important part in hunting rituals even in prehistoric times. The Celts worshipped the horned god Cernunnos (right), while later British legend remembered the antlered figure of Herne the Hunter. Harts – male red deer – were emblems of nobility in heraldic days, while stags retained from early times an image of virility that was celebrated in the Victorian era by Landseer's famous painting *The Monarch of the Glen*.

legend Vishnu took the guise of the boar Varaha to dive into the abyssal depths and rescue the Earth from the demonic Hiranyaksha, while the Norse god Freyr rode on Gullinbursti, a boar with golden bristles fashioned by the dwarves.

Lamb

An image of innocence and purity foredestined to an early death, the lamb was a natural symbol of Jesus Christ, called by John the Baptist (according to St John's Gospel) "the Lamb of God, who takes away the sin of the world".

Fox

Despite the insistence by shepherds and hunters that foxes are vermin, most cultures had a nuanced approach to them. "Crafty as a fox," people said, and there was always a sneaking respect, as well as righteous indignation, for these domestic predators living outside the law. Popular anti-heroes of North American trickster tales, foxes featured in Japanese legend as *kitsune*, shapeshifters that took the form of beautiful women to drain men of their vital essence. And when medieval satirists wanted to lampoon the ruling class of churchmen, knights and lawyers, they did so through the figure of Reynard the Fox, endlessly subverting the established order.

Dog

Man's best friend received a mixed press in the world's symbology. Contemptuous references, particularly in Middle and Far Eastern sources, contrasted with images of loyalty, like Greyfriars Bobby or

the dog that brought bread daily to St Roch as he lay in the wilderness, sick with plague. The canine presence in myth most often took the form of guard dogs, emblems of ferociously protective vigilance; three-headed Cerberus watched over the entrance to the Classical Underworld, while in Norse legend Garm was the original hound of Hel.

Cat

Cats had largely feminine associations, whether in the adjective "catty" or in their traditional role as witches' familiars. More positively, they had enduring links with grace and beauty. Ancient Egyptians worshipped the cat-headed goddess Bastet, and the gigantic Cat of Heliopolis guarded the sun god Ra on his nocturnal journey through the Underworld from the attacks of the chaos-serpent Apophis.

Pig

Pigs were traditionally vilified as emblems of greed. Considered unclean in Jewish and Islamic tradition, they became symbols of gluttony and sloth for the medieval bestiarists. The pork-eating Chinese took a more benevolent view; a pig under a roof was the initial ideogram for the concept of "home".

Elephant

Imposing, gentle and reliable, elephants in India served as the mounts of maharajahs and gods, notably thunder-bearing Indra. The elephant-headed deity Ganesha was always popular, noted for his kindness and wisdom.

UNICORN According to legend this horned hybrid could be captured only by a virgin. In her company, the wild beast became meek. As such, the unicorn symbolizes male and female chastity through the idea of a love not consummated.

Monkey

Fascinating to humans as a distorted self-image, monkeys were usually deemed tricksters and mischief-makers. Hanuman, one of the protagonists of India's great epic the *Ramayana*, was a humanoid monkey. He in turn probably provided the inspiration for Sun Wukong, the Monkey King hero of the novel *Journey to the West* (often known in the West simply as *Monkey*), a classic of Chinese literature.

Bull

Like the boar, the bull was traditionally an emblem of uncontrollable force, as the phrase "a bull in a china shop" suggests. Yet their sheer power and economic importance ensured them a leading place in myth; the principal gods of most of the nations of the Fertile Crescent had links to bulls. In Hindu tradition the sacred bull Nandi was Shiva's mount and the chief of his attendants, while Persian Mithraists venerated a primeval bull whose semen fecundated the entire world. Zeus took bull form to ravish Europa, and Queen Pasiphaë of Crete mated with a bull to produce the hybrid Minotaur.

Cow

The symbolism of the placid cow could hardly have been more different from that of the rampant and destructive bull, but both reflected in their separate ways images of fecundity. The cow was the gentle life-giver whose milk in Norse myth fed the primordial frost-giant Ymir, and it was venerated in Buddhist and Jainist tradition as well as in Hinduism for its long-suffering patience and equanimity.

REPTILES AND INSECTS

Creatures of hidden places

BUTTERFLY
Delicate and beautiful, butterflies symbolized the soul in lands as far apart as Mesoamerica and Japan. New Zealand Maoris and the Nagas of Assam both believed that the spirits of dead people returned to earth in butterfly form. In Christianity the butterfly symbolizes resurrection.

In comparison with mammals and birds, most reptiles and insects were poorly viewed in myth, often treated with a distaste bordering on revulsion. Toads featured as witches' familiars, lizards and scorpions signified barrenness and desolation, and in the Judaeo-Christian tradition at least snakes took on an aura of positive evil: "That old serpent, who is called the Devil and Satan". Yet some creatures bucked the trend. Bees were famously busy and productive, and the biblical Book of Proverbs recommended to lazy individuals "Go to the ant, O sluggard. Consider her ways and be wise". Even snakes had their admirers: the Rainbow Serpent of Aborigine lore helped shape the landscape of Outback Australia, and the *naga*s of India were guardian figures controlling hidden reserves of power and wealth.

Snake

Snakes haunted people's imaginations from the earliest times, and a complex symbolism developed around them. Figures of evil in the Christian tradition because of their connection with the serpent in the Garden of Eden, they were viewed more positively in other cultures, sometimes even as guardian figures; snakes featured on the *caduceus*, or winged wand of the Roman god Mercury, and on the rod of Asclepius, deity of healing (see pages 88–89). The snake-bodied *naga*s of Indian myth lived in magnificent underwater palaces and were regarded

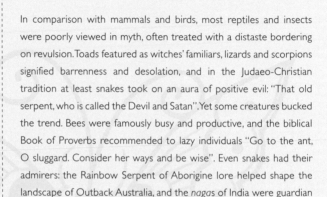

with respect, if not affection, while the Aztec plumed serpent was only the greatest of many Mesoamerican serpentine gods. Snakes' ability to slough their skin attracted attention, suggesting a link with rejuvenation; a superstition held that eating a snake could restore a person's youth. Snake cults were found around the world, sometimes with a distinctly phallic element. Yet there was also a widespread association with envy, jealousy and deceit; North American peoples accused liars of speaking with forked tongues and in the world's oldest literary work, the *Epic of Gilgamesh*, a snake stole the plant of immortality that the hero had laboured to discover.

Dragon

Primeval products of the human imagination, dragons were familiar around the world, although their symbolism differed widely from land to land. In general, oriental dragons were creatures of power

THE VIRTUOUS BEE

A universal emblem of industry, the bee also had imperial connotations. Napoleon adopted the insect as his personal emblem, following the example of France's early Merovingian and Carolingian kings. An ancient tradition held that bees settling on the mouth of an infant in its cradle guaranteed future eloquence: Plato was called the Athenian Bee for this reason, and similar stories were told of Sophocles. The orderly nature of the hive, the social organization of its occupants and their production of the healthy honeycomb made beehives – symbol of St Ambrose – a popular metaphor for Christian monastic communities. Tales from around the world, from North America to Japan, presented bees as helpers in time of trouble, swarming to attack any enemies who threatened.

that, if treated with respect, could be benevolent protectors. In the heavens dragons were regarded as rain-bringers, while on Earth they became an imperial symbol (left) – China's emperors sat on the Dragon Throne. In Classical myth dragons were fearsome and vigilant guardians of treasure – the name came from the Greek *drakos*, meaning "eye" – confronted by heroes like Jason and Herakles. Drawing on the Book of Revelation's red dragon with seven heads and 10 horns, the Christian tradition regarded the beasts as demonic, prey for dragon-slayers like St Michael and St George.

Tortoise

A byword for slowness and patience in the West, as in the story of its race with the hare, the tortoise occupied a grander position in Eastern myth, where it personified reliability and strength. In China the Black Tortoise was one of four symbols of the constellations (see page 111), while in Hindu cosmology the tortoise Chukwa bore on its back the elephant that supported the world.

Toad

Long regarded as ugliness personified, the harmless toad endured a wretched symbolic fate as the creature of witches and sorcerers. One ancient superstition held that toads were poisonous; the original "toadies" or toad-eaters were quack medicine-sellers'

THE OUROBOROS

From the Greek for "tail-devourer", the word "ouroboros" referred to a snake or dragon looped in a circle with its tail in its mouth. The image was found in mythology around the world, from Central America to Europe, Africa and India – one of the best-known examples being Jormungandr, the Norse world serpent that grew to encircle the Earth. The symbol also fascinated philosophers and mystics, who saw in it an image of life that continually renews itself from its own resources (this engraving is from Johann Daniel Mylius's *Anatomia auri*, 1628). Dahomean legend had a more sinister take on the same theme. Their world serpent, Aido Hwedo, was said to be living off the Earth's mineral resources, but when they were finally used up would instead devour itself, tail first, bringing on the end of the world.

assistants who purported to swallow live toads in order to be miraculously revived by the cure-all concoction. On a more positive note, toads were also sometimes thought to have medicinal uses, on the homeopathic principle that a very small amount of a harmful substance could produce a beneficial effect. Even more bizarrely, they were popularly reputed to have jewels in their foreheads.

Scorpion

Synonymous with malice and envy for its venom, the scorpion was also thought to produce an antidote for the ills it caused. In the words of the 17th-century satirist Samuel Butler: "Tis true a scorpion's oil is said/To cure the wounds the venom made".

CREATURES OF THE AIR

Winged intermediaries of the gods

FALCON
Symbol of Horus, this predatory lord of the skies was famed for its keen eyesight and lethal stoop. Falcons were symbols of vigilance and aggression.

The heavens were traditionally seen as the realm of the gods, so the creatures that inhabited them were often accorded a spiritual dimension. Souls were sometimes shown in Christian iconography with wings, as were angels and other semi-divine beings. In the Classical world too, Romans looked to the sky and to the flight of birds to decode the heavens' will through augury. Long before the age of aviation, shamans donned feathered costumes to take soul journeys. In general birds represented the element of air: light, ethereal and touched with celestial splendour.

Eagle

The eagle ruled the skies much as the lion was king of mammals, so it comes as no surprise that both shared similar associations with royalty and empire. Eagles served as emblems for the Byzantine Empire, imperial France and Russia, Germany, Austro-Hungary and Prussia, and the Bald eagle is the symbol of the USA. In myth the bird was associated with Zeus and Jupiter and appeared on the standards of the Roman legions; at emperors' funerals an eagle was released from the pyre to symbolize the dead ruler's passage to the afterlife. In Christian art the eagle represents St John the Evangelist, hence its frequent appearance on church lecterns. "Eagle eyes" have symbolized keen vision at

least since Old Testament times, when Job in the book of that name remarked of the bird that its "eyes behold far off".

Raven

Few birds carried a more complex and contradictory symbolism than the raven, seen both as a symbol of destruction and a protective spirit. Edgar Allan Poe's poem of that name summed up the bird's long-standing reputation as a harbinger of doom. The tradition itself dated back at least to Roman times, when ravens were  said to have predicted the death of both Julius Caesar and the Emperor Augustus; one was even said to have entered the orator Cicero's house on the day of his murder, disarranging the coverlets on his bed. The bird's prophetic aspect was recognized by the ancient Greeks, who made it sacred to Apollo, and later to the Arabs, who nicknamed it *abu zajir*, father of omens.

Both Scandinavian and Celtic myth associated ravens with battles, no doubt because of their appetite for carrion. The Celtic war goddess the Morrigan sometimes took raven form on the battlefield, while the Norse deity Odin relied on two ravens, Hugin and Munin, to act as his spies, reporting to him all that happened in the world. Yet the birds also had a more positive symbolism, based chiefly on their intelligence and cunning. The ravens at the Tower of London are considered to this day protective birds whose presence guarantees the national well-being; they supposedly trace their lineage back to Bran the Blessed (the name means "raven"), a Welsh hero whose head (according to the *Mabinogion*) was buried at the Tower.

In the Bible ravens fed the prophet Elijah in the wilderness, while in the legends of America's North Pacific Coast Raven was a trickster culture hero (see illustration, page 55), famed for his voracious appetites, who shaped the landscape and provided most of the necessities on which humans depend for their survival.

Peacock

For the author of the *Physiologus*, the chief inspiration for the medieval bestiaries, the peacock with its glorious tail display was an emblem of vanity. The symbolism was duly taken up by monarchs eager to show off their own magnificence, and until the revolution of 1979 the shahs of Persia sat on the Peacock Throne. The greatest of the seven holy beings venerated by the Kurdish Yazidis of Iraq was the Peacock Angel.

PEACOCK
Some traditions associated the decorations on the peacock's tail with vigilance or even with the Evil Eye, and in many European countries it was considered bad luck to have a peacock feather in the home.

OWL OF ERUDITION

The wise old owl was Athene's bird, sacred to the Greek goddess of knowledge and adopted as the emblem of Athens, the city dedicated in her name. Even today, scholars may be characterized as "owlish". Elsewhere, however, the bird's reputation was less auspicious. Its nocturnal habits, predatory lifestyle and haunting cry all led it to be associated with death, and it was generally considered a bird of ill omen, listed among the unclean fowl in the Book of Leviticus. In Europe owls sometimes served as witches' familiars, while in parts of Africa they were linked to sorcerers. Ancient Romans regarded the birds as particularly baleful. An owl supposedly entered Commodus's room shortly before he was assassinated.

Vulture

Almost universally regarded as a bird of ill omen whose presence betokened death, the vulture had more positive attributes in ancient Egypt. There the bird was personified as Nekhbet, patroness of Upper Egypt, and her protective image regularly appeared on the pharaoh's double crown.

Crane

Graceful birds famed for their elaborate mating rituals, cranes were mostly seen as auspicious presences. In the Far East they were symbols of longevity (at right is a Japanese *mon* or crest), and in China it was claimed that the Immortals of Taoist legend travelled on cranes across the heavens. They were also associated with fidelity for their custom of retaining the same mate for many years, if not for life. In Western bestiaries they won a reputation for vigilance, from a story from Pliny that sentry cranes stood guard at night with a pebble clutched in a raised claw; if they fell asleep, they were woken by the sound of splashing.

Crow

As fellow corvids, crows share many of the qualities of ravens, including their coal-black hue, and they traditionally conveyed a similarly divergent symbolism. Like ravens, they were often seen as birds of ill omen; the poison-pen letter-writers who from time to time plagued French villages were often dubbed The Crow, after Henri-Georges Clouzot's wartime film of that name. The association with battlefields also carried over, as in the border ballad of *The*

BAT
In China bats were associated with good luck and happiness: five bats shown as a group represented respectively the blessings of health, wealth, love of virtue, old age and a natural death.

Twa Corbies, in which two crows discussed how best to dispose of the body of a new-slain knight. Yet the more benign aspects also fed through. For the Chipewayan people of Arctic Canada, Crow played a similar role to that of Raven in the tales of their West Coast neighbours. Chinese myth described how in early times supranatural crows carried no fewer than 10 separate suns across the Earth on a rotational basis. It was left to the makers of the cartoon film *Dumbo* to create the streetwise crow, updating the image of the intelligent, opportunistic bird for modern times.

Magpie

Cousin of the crow and raven, the magpie also inspired mixed emotions. Generally considered unlucky in the West and often condemned for its pilfering habits, as in Rossini's *Thieving Magpie*, the bird was also reluctantly admired for its ingenuity, rather in the manner of the fox. In contrast, the brilliantly-coloured magpies of the Far East were usually viewed as propitious, and they crop up to this day on greeting cards as emblems of good luck and good fortune.

Cock

The national emblem of France, the cock was generally seen as a symbol of vigilance, keeping watch for the dawn. Its cry reached the spirit world, for ghosts and vampires took flight before cockcrow. Dedicated to Apollo in Classical times because of their connection with the rising sun, the birds also served as a symbol of masculinity; bridegrooms in Hungary used to carry them to church before a wedding. In Christian tradition cocks frequently appeared on weathervanes on church steeples, symbolically summoning the faithful to worship; an Islamic tradition maintained that when the great cock in the First Heaven ceased to crow, the Day of Judgment would be at hand.

Swan

The very image of beauty and grace, swans found their way into folklore in tales of swan maidens – lovely women who put on feathered finery to take swan form. An ancient legend insisted that swans sang once in their lives as a sign of approaching death – the notion that lay behind the phrase "swan song", describing a final performance. In almost all lands where it was known, the swan was an emblem of loveliness, whether spiritual – in India mystics  were sometimes called Paramahamsa or "Supreme Swan" – or artistic, as the symbol of the Modernismo movement in Latin American poetry or in Ben Jonson's description of Shakespeare as the Swan of Avon.

Bat

Sharing the owl's dislike for daylight, bats found themselves tarred with the same superstitious brush; dead bats, like dead owls, were sometimes nailed to barn doors to scare off evil spirits. The blood-feeding vampire bats of South America further darkened the animals' reputation, and in the Mayan supernatural epic the *Popol Vuh* a death bat decapitated one of the Hero Twins on a visit to the Underworld. Yet some cultures took a more favourable view: Tongans treated bats with respect as reincarnations of dead souls, while in China they were associated with good luck and happiness.

WATER CREATURES

Denizens of the deep

COWRIE
Femininity
and fertility
are conjured
up by the
cowrie shell,
the decorative
use of which
sometimes
serves to
signify love.

The waters are the least charted part of the Earth's surface; parts of the oceans and of some lakes remain relatively little known to this day. So the symbolism of the creatures that live in them remained darker and more opaque than the imagery associated with the beasts with whom people shared the land. An aura of mystery surrounded the denizens of the deep, and tales of sea serpents and monsters stretched back to the earliest times. Yet fish also became a symbol of Christ, the fisher of souls, and individual species too had positive connotations: the Celts told tales of the Salmon of Wisdom, while the carp was an image of good fortune and longevity in the Far East.

Salmon

In the tales told by peoples of America's North Pacific Coast, Salmon Boy was a hero, for the salmon was admired as a symbol of courage and persistence, battling as it does to return to its native river to spawn. Some similar logic may have underlain Irish tales of the Salmon of Wisdom, implying that knowledge too was only attained by long and patient effort.

SCALLOP
The scallop
shell was the
symbol of
pilgrims making
their way to
the shrine of
St James at
Santiago de
Compostela in
northwestern
Spain.

Carp

Carp can live for up to 65 years, so it is no surprise that they became symbols of longevity in China. They can also leap as much as 3m (10ft) high, giving rise to the saying "Carp jumps over the Dragon Gate", applied to someone of humble station gaining an unexpected honour.

Koi – a domesticated variety of the Common carp – are popular ornamental fish, above all in Japan, where they are associated with love and friendship.

Whale

One likely origin for the biblical Leviathan, the whale also entered Old Testament legend as the creature that swallowed the prophet Jonah, who spent three days in its belly before being spewed out. Meanwhile the hunting of whales spawned an elaborate ritual, particularly among the coastal Inuit, who relied on the beasts as a vital source of food and oil. Much care was taken to propitiate the prey animals, by songs, incantations and ritual enactments of the hunt. After one had been killed, its carcass would be welcomed ashore with singing and dancing, and the community would observe three days of mourning to placate the whale's spirit before they feasted.

Dolphin

Famously friendly to humans, dolphins appeared in artwork from Minoan Crete, and a well-known Greek legend told how the poet Arion threw himself into the sea to escape from pirates and was carried back to land by a dolphin. The creatures also served as messengers for the sea god Poseidon. In India the legendary *makara* that was used as a mount by Ganga, goddess of the Ganges River, was sometimes depicted as a river dolphin. South American tales described the *boto* or Amazon river dolphin as a shapeshifter that could take human form to mate with women and sire children.

STONES AND MINERALS

Assets from the earth

IRON
Wellington was the Iron Duke, Bismarck the Iron Chancellor and Thatcher the Iron Lady. A common element in the Earth's crust, the metal stood metaphorically for anything strong, effective, unyielding and inflexible – qualities that might be admired but were rarely loved.

For many ancient cultures stones and minerals were the handiwork of the gods and so retained a numinous quality from their suprahuman origins. The Inca and other Andean peoples venerated *huacas*, natural shrines that often took the form of bare outcrops of rock. Precious stones were even more highly prized as evidence of a divine delight in crafting objects of beauty. Metals gained value in relation to their rarity, so copper and its alloy, bronze, were generally more esteemed than iron. For the Chinese, jade represented longevity, and prominent individuals were at one stage buried in suits of the precious green stone in the hope of prolonging their spiritual existence. But no substance could rival the worldwide prestige of gold, the metal of majesty whose sheen emulated the sun's radiance.

Gold

The Aztecs called it *teocuitlatl*, the excrement of the gods, and linked this most precious of metals with the Sun, an association also made by medieval European alchemists. Otherwise, gold's symbolism split two ways. On the one hand it expresses supreme glory, as in Olympic gold medals or the various golden ages that have graced human history. On the other it was associated with greed and false gods, as in the biblical image of the Golden Calf. The Roman naturalist Pliny, who recorded with scorn that Mark Antony habitually relieved himself in golden chamber pots, expressed the hostile view in claiming that "the first person to put gold on his fingers committed the worst crime against human life".

THE FLAMING PEARL

A frequent image in Chinese art was a dragon pursuing a pearl giving off flamelike swirls of light. The Tang-era (618–907CE) motif (right) seems to have come from Central Asia. Western scholars used to see celestial symbolism in the emblem, believing it represented a sky dragon swallowing the Moon, signifying an eclipse. Eastern interpreters tended rather to view the pearl as a spiritual emblem, representing spiritual perfection for Taoists and transcendental wisdom for Buddhists and Hindus. In the popular imagination the flaming pearl took on a simpler significance as the Pearl of Potentiality, a gem that could grant wishes and that had the power to multiply itself endlessly.

Diamond

Diamonds, the hardest of natural materials, took their name from the Greek *adamas*, "invincible". Even so, Pliny had the curious notion that they dissolved in goat's blood. For the Romans they were the most precious of all luxuries and most other cultures also accorded them a high place, although in Persia they were considered unlucky. In India the gems often served for eyes in statues of the gods. The *vajra* or thunderbolt wielded by the Hindu god Indra literally meant "diamond", while the world's oldest printed book, a 9th-century Chinese edition of the Buddhist *Diamond Sutra*, was so called because the text was intended to serve as a "diamond blade to cut through worldly illusion". In the West they became the stone of choice for engagement rings for their durability, which not only suggested marital constancy but more practically meant that the stones retained their value.

IMPLEMENTS

Everyday objects that acquired special meaning

KEY
A traditional symbol of authority, keys are presented to newly elected popes in memory of Jesus' promise to Peter that "I will give you the keys of the kingdom of Heaven".

Fairly obviously, the symbolic value of man-made implements came mostly from the uses to which they were put. The extraordinary veneration accorded to the Holy Grail in medieval times, for example, stemmed from the belief that Jesus had drunk from it at the Last Supper. In other contexts, however, the cup shape could be a simple image of conviviality, with no more resonance than the crossed knife and fork and teacup logos that appear on motorway information panels to indicate a nearby service station. In general, the utensils that carried the strongest associative message were those that came to be linked with basic human qualities: a ladder for aspiration, an anchor for firmness of purpose, scales for balanced justice.

Cup

"My cup runneth over. Surely goodness and mercy shall follow me all the days of my life." As the psalm suggested, a full cup was a potent symbol of repletion and of all that life could offer. In contrast, an overturned cup indicated emptiness and the vanity of sensual pleasure. Cups also stood for conviviality ("the cup of good cheer"), and in recent times became associated with victory as the prize of choice for sporting events, from school sports days all the way up to the FIFA World Cup.

Compasses

Compasses shared something of scales' symbolism, in their case implying reason and measure. The Romantic William Blake satirized the image in his famous engraving of Sir Isaac Newton, showing a naked figure representing the scientist using compasses in an ultimately futile attempt to quantify God's limitless creation.

Bell

Bells have had ritual significance from early times, being used to signal the start of religious ceremonies at least from Assyrian days. They have also long been considered consecrated instruments with the power to drive away evil spirits. In Siberia shamans regularly wore bells to protect them on spirit journeys; in western Europe it was claimed that the sound of church bells drove the trolls out of Scandinavia and caused flying witches to fall from the sky. For many centuries a "passing bell" was rung as individuals lay dying to protect them from demons as well as to encourage passers-by to pray for their souls. Church bells were also sometimes sounded to banish plague or to cause storms to abate. In the days when clocks were scarce, bells marked the passage of time; and while the tolling knell gave notice of deaths and funerals, happy peals announced christenings and marriages.

Yoke

Armies conquered by Rome were forced to march under three spears, two upright and one set across, "passing under the yoke" to express submission. Even since that time the implement has been the ultimate symbol of defeat and subjection, associated with slavery as well as with military defeat. When the prophet Jeremiah opined that "It is good for a man that he bear the yoke in his youth", he was expressing the view that humility can help prepare the soul to receive God.

Scales

Scales are the main insignia of justice around the world, suggesting the careful weighing of evidence involved in conducting a fair trial. The association goes back at least as far as Roman times, when Justitia, goddess of justice, was shown blindfolded (to indicate her impartiality) and clutching a sword and scales. Even further back in time, a similar image had suggested the fate of the human soul in the hands of the gods. Ancient Egyptian imagery from the Book of the Dead showed a judgment scene in which the heart of the deceased was weighed against a feather representing truth in the presence of the dread judge Osiris. If the heart proved the lighter of the two, the dead person could pass on into the company of the gods, but if it was heavier he or she was consumed for all eternity by a crocodile-headed monster. A similar thought informed the biblical writing on the wall that foretold the downfall of King Belshazzar of Babylon: "Thou art weighed in the balance and found wanting".

Anchor

St Paul described hope as "a sure and steadfast anchor of the soul", reflecting the implement's significance as an emblem of security and stability. In early Christian times the anchor also served as a *crux dissimulata*, a disguised cross whose cruciform shape was recognized by believers but evaded their Roman persecutors.

Lyre

The lyre is the oldest of all stringed instruments, featuring on Sumerian monuments dating back 5,000 years. The earliest examples were large, towering over the players who sat before them, but smaller, portable lyres appeared in Egypt from about 1000BCE on. In Classical Greece the lyre was the instrument of Apollo, in whose hands it became a symbol of the magic power of music; legend claimed that the god played on one when Troy was being built and the stones danced into their allotted positions of their own accord. Orpheus used his lyre to entrance the birds and beasts and even to soften the heart of the dread Hades himself; Arion played so enticingly that a dolphin rose from the deep to rescue him when he was cast into the sea by pirates. Even now lyres can often be seen in concert-hall festoons representing the triumph of harmony.

THE HOLY GRAIL

No trophy was ever more ardently sought than the Holy Grail, said to be the chalice employed at the Last Supper and subsequently used to collect the blood of Christ at the Crucifixion. According to one common version of the story, Joseph of Arimathea then carried the Grail to Britain; another held that angels brought it from Heaven to a mountaintop stronghold, where it was guarded by a sworn brotherhood of knights. The mission undertaken by knights of King Arthur's court to find it became the great fictional narrative of the Middle Ages. Today the word "grail" is used metaphorically to describe any long-sought goal involving dedication and effort, particularly if the quest has a spiritual as well as a practical dimension.

WEAPONS

A panoply of arms

Weapons were first and foremost symbols of power, reflecting the authority conceded to *force majeure* through most of human history. Thor's hammer and Neptune's trident stood, like the swords wielded by innumerable sculpted kings, for dominion through might. Yet some arms transcended their violent origins to represent wider principles guaranteed by the threat of duress, like the arrow of truth or the sword of justice. And non-violence also had identifying images of its own, from the broken arrow and calumet to the familiar circular logo of the Campaign for Nuclear Disarmament, adopted by peace campaigners everywhere.

Sword

Across Eurasia swords were until recently the prime symbol of war. "Fire and the sword" meant military devastation, while "to put to the sword" was to kill. Someone girding on their sword was preparing for battle, while returning the sword to the sheath indicated peace was at hand – maybe even that a time might be coming to turn swords into ploughshares, as foreseen in the biblical Book of Isaiah. Most heroes of legend had their own special sword – Arthur's was Excalibur, Roland's Durandel – while the real-life samurai warriors of Japan

viewed their blades as their most prized possessions. Yet the sword also had wider symbolic meanings. It could be the arm of truth cutting through falsehood; St Paul described God's word as "the sword of the spirit". Statues of Lady Justice showed her carrying a sword to punish evil-doers.

Arrow

American myth in particular associated arrows with thunderstorms. Mesoamerican sky god Mixcoatl carried a bundle of arrows, perhaps because he was also linked with hunting, while the Cheyenne of the Great Plains guarded four sacred medicine arrows, said to have been theirs since the creation of the world. Broken arrows signified peace, while Cupid's darts stood for the pain that love could cause. When William Blake called for his "arrows of desire", he was demanding tools to help him to create an English Jerusalem.

Bow

When Ulysses returned to Ithaca after two decades away fighting the Trojan War, he used his old bow to prove his identity. Only he was able to fire an arrow through the loops on a dozen axe handles; none of his wife's unwanted suitors even managed to string the bow. Bows were generally associated with strength and skill, although the unknown warrior who killed Ahab of Israel in the biblical Book of Kings did so merely by drawing his bow "at a venture". To have two strings to one's bow was a wise precaution against an emergency.

Trident

The trident was indelibly linked with the Roman sea god Neptune. The figure of Britannia, adopted as an emblem of the British Empire, deliberately harked back to the deity to invoke British sea power alongside the nation's imperial ambitions.

EMBLEMS OF AUTHORITY

Temporal power and its trappings

CROZIER
A staff with a shepherd's crook at its tip, the crozier served in the Christian world as a symbol of Church dignitaries' pastoral role as shepherds to their flocks.

One of the defining trends of modern political life has been the desacralization of power. The discreet business suits and first-name forms of address favoured by modern democratic leaders are a far cry from the splendour of early monarchs – from the Muisca heirs of what is now upland Colombia, who were coated from head to foot in gold dust on their accession, to the pharaohs of ancient Egypt, worshipped as earthly gods. The symbols of secular majesty were also translated to the celestial sphere, and the panoply of thrones, crowns and sceptres adopted by temporal kings were imagined to adorn the deities in Heaven.

Rod

Royal sceptres (see pages 72–73) were sophisticated refinements of the humbler rod or staff traditionally associated with lesser grades of authority. Of the two, staffs had gentler connotations, linking them to people travelling by foot, notably pilgrims and oriental monks. In contrast, rods suggested punishment: "Spare the rod and spoil the child"; "Kiss the rod"; or, as Jehovah told the king of Israel in the psalm, "You shall break them with a rod of iron". A more positive take on rods came from their association with living trees. There was a tradition in Germany for young people on certain feast days to playfully scourge members of the opposite sex with "rods of life" – freshly cut budding boughs – in the belief that they conferred health, energy and fertility. In the Bible, Aaron's rod flowered and brought forth almonds as a divinely-inspired sign that he and his tribe were the legitimate high priests of Israel.

Crown

The ultimate mark of royalty, the crown owed its primacy to the head's role as seat of the brain, the wellspring of all human activity. The tradition dated back at least to the first pharaohs, who wore an elaborate double crown symbolizing their rule over both Upper and Lower Egypt. Elsewhere, the original crowns may have been open-topped diadems, themselves a development of the custom of adorning people with wreaths. The

THE CAP OF LIBERTY

Contemporary illustrations of the French Revolution show working-class street fighters wearing a distinctive red cap. Floppy in texture, it was easily recognized from its drooping tip, hanging down to the front or side. Known at the time as the liberty bonnet, it drew on memories of ancient Rome, where just such a cap had been worn by freedmen – slaves emancipated by their masters and granted citizenship. The headgear originated in Phrygia, a kingdom in central Anatolia, and

it appeared in earlier Greek art as the mark of someone foreign and exotic. Much later the Phrygian cap, as it became known, was adopted as a symbol of American independence by forces fighting the British crown. Displayed on top of a "liberty pole" in a town or village, it served as a public declaration of revolutionary intent. French volunteers who fought alongside Washington's armies took the emblem home, and to this day Marianne, the national symbol of France, is often shown wearing a liberty cap.

Romans had a gradation of eight different crowns, ranging from simple garlands of wild flowers up to golden coronets, to reward different degrees of military achievement. Like other emblems of power, crowns conferred cares as well as glory. Shakespeare made the stresses of high office one of his main themes, coining the phrase "the hollow crown" to describe the uncertainties of rule and making Henry IV memorably remark: "Uneasy lies the head that wears a crown". A coronet could even be made an instrument of mockery, as when Roman soldiers made a crown of thorns for Jesus at the time of the Crucifixion, ironically hailing him as king of the Jews.

Flail

The pharaohs of ancient Egypt used to carry a crook and a threshing flail as emblems of their authority. Elsewhere in Africa fly-whisks were symbols of monarchy; Jomo Kenyatta, the founder of modern Kenya, carried one as a traditional Maasai emblem of power.

FLAIL
The pharaohs' use of the crook and flail in ancient Egypt indicated their role as guarantors of the people's food supply, pastoral and arable.

Sceptre

Portia in The Merchant of Venice said of rulers, "His sceptre shows the force of temporal power,/The attribute to awe and majesty/ Wherein doth sit the dread and fear of kings." It was left to the Cavalier dramatist James Shirley to spell out the limitations of power: "Sceptre and crown/Must tumble down,/And in the dust be equal made/With the poor crooked scythe and spade". As symbols of majesty, sceptres could equally well illustrate the glories or the downfall of high estate. In myth, Agamemnon bore a staff of office shaped by Hephaestos, the god of craftsmen and metallurgy, and successively owned by Zeus, Hermes, and the kings Pelops, Atreus and Thyestes. The *vajra* ("thunderbolt") held by Hindu priests during religious ceremonies, and the equivalent Tibetan *dorje*, were both often referred to as small sceptres. To this day the bejewelled golden sceptre of the British monarchs is topped by a cross and orb (illustration, right), which represents the globe, mounted above the celebrated Culinnan I diamond, taken from the largest gem-quality diamond ever discovered.

Throne

Literally the seat of regal might, the throne in time became synonymous with the office of kingship; those who visualized God as a heavenly monarch generally pictured him seated on a celestial throne. Solomon sat on a throne of ivory overlaid with gold that was approached up six steps, for one function of thrones through the ages has been to raise the occupants physically above the level of those around them. Such exaltation was not for the plain-speaking Samuel Johnson, who took the view that the throne of human felicity was a tavern chair.

Girdle

A girdle was an ancient emblem of fidelity, perhaps recalling the belt made for Venus by her husband Vulcan, which fell off as she dallied with the war god Mars. In later times belts were sometimes claimed to provide protection against witches, while ones blessed by a priest purportedly guaranteed to ease the labour of childbirth.

LIGHT AND FIRE

The imagery of illumination

"And God said, 'Let there be light'; and there was light." The symbolism of illumination was far-reaching, covering spiritual as well as physical revelation, and it almost always had positive connotations, drawing as it did on the primordial radiance of the Sun. Fire shared some of the same prestige, although the brightness of flames could also have a threatening or destructive aspect. Cinders or ashes, reflections of mortality in many cultures, signified the fate of those consumed by too much heat and light.

NIMBUS
This aureole of light that sometimes surrounds the Sun or Moon is caused by the refraction of light through mist. An association between light and divinity led to the use of nimbuses and haloes to indicate the sanctity of figures such as Christian saints.

FLAME

For many peoples in many different lands, flames were an agent of purification, burning away blemishes and sins. Zoroastrian fire worship seems to have grown out of the early Persian custom of ordeal by heat. Those who survived the trial were not only absolved of any crime but also emerged physically and mentally strengthened, a claim also made for modern fire-walkers. In Jewish and Christian belief God sometimes spoke from fire – Moses' burning 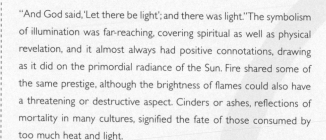 bush was but one example – while in Chinese and Muslim art a flame sometimes served to represent the divine presence. In the secular world flames have long been used to symbolize physical passion, a sentiment preserved in the phrase "an old flame". For alchemists, fire was an agent of transformation vital to the creation of the Philosopher's Stone; for the apocalyptically minded, it was the agent of destruction that one day would consume the Earth.

Torch

A beacon of freedom in the hand of the Statue of Liberty, a torch symbolically was a flame raised high for all to see. Reviving an ancient tradition, the modern Olympic torch signifies the ideals of chivalry, sportsmanship and striving for excellence, and "passing the torch" has come to mean the handing on of any high ambition.

Dawn

A universal symbol of hope and fresh starts, the dawn marked the return of light as the night's darkness was dispelled. Japan appropriated the image for its rising-sun motif, also reflected in its name of Nippon (literally "the Sun's origin"), which referred to the island nation's easterly location in relation to China and Eurasia.

Ashes

"Ashes to ashes and dust to dust," English clergymen say when burying the dead, emphasizing ashes' role as an image of the vanity of human illusions. Around the world ashes were symbols of humility and abasement, from the Old Testament custom of donning sackcloth and ashes in penitence to the Brahman custom of rubbing the body with ashes in preparation for religious ceremonies. Hindu yogi sometimes appeared naked but for ashes to signify their contempt for the material world. There was also a long-standing connection with death and mourning; ancient Egyptians and Greeks all heaped ashes on their heads as a mark of grief. In the 20th century the American poet Carl Sandburg asked rhetorically, "What is the past but a bucket of ashes?", and today Catholic priests still mark the foreheads of penitents with ashes on Ash Wednesday, the first day of Lent.

TIME AND DEATH
Mementoes of mortality

Mortality had one of the world's most instantly recognizable symbolic repertoires, replete with bones, skulls and skeletons. Time too, which led individuals toward death, acquired a familiar imagery of sundials and hourglasses, most of them signalling a *memento mori* awareness of the transience of human and animal existence. In Hindu and Buddhist cultures the Wheel of Life, turning through the cycle of birth and dying, conveyed our impermanence while also carrying the message of rebirth through reincarnation.

Father Time

Usually shown with a long white beard and holding an hourglass, Father Time traced his origins back to the Roman god Saturn and his Greek predecessor Kronos, both associated with time and shown carrying a sickle. The figure came to represent the Old Year in New Year's Eve celebrations, supplanted by a baby when midnight sounded.

Hourglass

Designed to permit sand to flow from one end to the other and then back again, hourglasses measured the passage of time and suggested its endless continuation. In the Hindu tradition Shiva possessed a similarly shaped drum, used for ritual purposes. In Tibetan Buddhism the drums were made of two human skulls, one male and the other female to ensure balanced *yin* and *yang*.

Skull

The skull served across cultures as a *memento mori* indicating the transitory nature of life. Golgotha, where Christ was crucified, meant "place of the skull", while a Christian hermit pictured with a skull signified the contemplation of death. Ancient Celts afforded cultic significance to human heads, believing they were the seat of the life-force, and in some non-Western cultures head-hunting was practised because the head was regarded as the repository of the soul. In pre-Columbian Mesoamerica human sacrifice was an important part of religious practice, and skulls adorned the grounds of many temple sites, such as Chichen Itza's sculpted "wall of skulls". The skull-and-crossbones symbol has long been used by soldiers in defiance of mortal danger (see box), and certain secret societies, such as the Skull and Bones at Yale University in the US, also use the motif.

DEATH OR GLORY

The motto of the Queen's Royal Lancers, and the accompanying skull-and-crossbones cap badge, date back to 1759. In that year the precursors of this British regiment, the 17th Lancers, won the name of the "Death or Glory Boys" in honour of their commanding officer General James Wolfe, who died leading his men to victory over the French at Quebec. The Lancers later matched defiant words to deeds when many of them rode to their deaths in the Charge of the Light Brigade at Balaclava in the Crimea in 1854.

Known as the *totenkopf*, the death's head motif was also used by cavalry in Prussia from the mid 1700s to 1918. A variant was resurrected in the 1930s, most notoriously by a Waffen-SS Panzergrenadier division. Some modern US reconnaissance battalions still informally sport the skull and crossbones, although now usually in honour of its familiar intimidatory use on pirate flags.

PART TWO

BELIEF SYSTEMS

- -

Symbols play a significant role in human affairs,
from politics to commerce. Yet they are most
central in belief systems. Almost all the world's
religions employ visual icons to convey spiritual
ideas. Societies and sects also use pictorial
imagery to embody core notions and bond their
members in a shared identity. The symbols may
even become objects of devotion, standing in
for the abstract concepts that they incarnate.

ANCIENT CIVILIZATIONS

Keepsakes of the earliest cultures

ANKH
The Egyptian hieroglyph that represents "life", the *ankh* remains a popular symbol today among neo-Pagans as well as with goths and hippies.

Easily memorable and endlessly suggestive, some symbols have a lifespan that outdates any other form of human communication. Images that were familiar to the earliest civilizations still put in an appearance today. Some preserve an aura of primeval mystery; others may be purely decorative, featuring as amulets, corporate logos, even tattoos. A few designs dating back to prehistoric times are also still recognizable now. The obese female figure known as the Venus of Willendorf may have been carved as early as 20,000BCE, but her rotund image still retains its power as a representation of fecundity identifiable as such around the globe.

Of the imagery of historic times, the iconography of ancient Egypt has become particularly familiar since the pharaonic civilization was rediscovered by the West in the 18th and 19th centuries. For all its influence on later cultures, Mesopotamia remains by comparison less remembered and less explored. Other worlds that have left a heritage of symbols include Minoan Crete and ancient Persia.

Aten

Depicted as a solar disk radiating rays of light, the *aten* was venerated as the representation of Egypt's only deity during the 14th-century BCE reign of the pharaoh Akhenaten, considered a heretic because of his monotheism. After the ruler's death, he and all his works were anathematized and the traditional, multitudinous pantheon was restored. The *aten* symbolized the life-giving energy flowing from Ra-Horus, the creator god, whose name was written in a cartouche like a pharaoh's to signify Ra's sovereign role as ruler of the universe.

THE PECTORAL OF THE TWIN GODDESSES

Found in the tomb of Tutankhamun, this chest decoration shows the young king as Osiris, protected by the wings of vulture-headed Nekhbet, protector of Upper Egypt, and Wadjet, cobra goddess of Lower Egypt. Osiris was god of the Underworld and the merciful bestower of eternal life. The pharaoh carries the crook and flail that served as the god's emblems of authority and wears the *atef* crown associated with his cult.

The *uraeuses* (1) at each side of the pectoral were associated with Wadjet (2) as well as with royal authority, represented by the pharaoh (3). The *ankh* (4) – here as a glyph meaning "life" – appears in the text panel adjoining the image of Nekhbet (5).

SCARAB
This symbol of transformation and renewal was used prominently in mummification ceremonies. A funerary scarab – placed on the chest of the dead to encourage rebirth of the soul – was discovered in the wrappings of Tutankhamun.

Scarab

An unlikely solar symbol, the humble dung-beetle was linked to Khepri, god of the rising sun. Much as the scarab rolls its ball of manure, so Khepri was thought to push the Sun through the Underworld each night before launching it on its daily journey across the heavens with the dawn. Just as the Sun was reborn daily, so the scarab itself was

PROTECTIVE POWERS

Many Egyptians wore amulets to ward off evil and bring happiness or good fortune. A talismanic necklace like this one (below) might have various tutelary motifs, usually including the *djed* pillar, representing the backbone of Osiris, and the *ankh*. Also featured here are cowrie shells, indicating female sexuality and fertility; fish, worn to ward off drowning; and the looped, *ankh*-like *sa* sign, the hieroglyph for "protection".

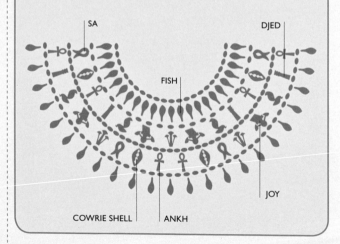

SA

DJED

FISH

JOY

COWRIE SHELL | ANKH

thought to be self-regenerating, born from animal carcasses or the dungballs where its larvae live. The insect therefore became a symbol of transformation and renewal.

Ankh

Originating as the hieroglyph representing "life", the *ankh* typically appears in ancient Egyptian artwork in the hands of a god or goddess thought to have the power to confer rebirth on a dead person's mummy. Modern theories of its origin range from the Freudian view that it represents stylized, superimposed female and male sexual organs to the suggestion that it imitated a sandal strap, the same hieroglyph standing for the words "life" and "sandal".

Uraeus

A stylized spitting cobra, the *uraeus* was the symbol of the goddess Wadjet, patroness of Lower Egypt – the region round the Nile Delta. As such, it featured on the headdresses of pharaohs to represent their rule over the area. It thus became an image of royal authority, conceived of as spitting venom at the ruler's enemies.

Sphinx

Some symbols travelled from one culture to another. The winged sphinx of Classical mythology (right) had its origins in an Egyptian predecessor, best known today from the Great Sphinx that stands guard over the pyramids of Giza. The Egyptian sphinx was a hybrid creature with the body of a lion and

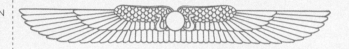

WINGED SUN
This symbol
(right) has
long been
associated in
the ancient
Near East
– from Egypt
to Persia
– with divinity,
royalty and
power.

the head of a ram, a falcon or a human being. Its function was as a spiritual watchdog providing protection against evil forces.

Feather of ma'at

One of the odder Egyptian symbols was the feather that represented *ma'at*, the concept of justice and good order, which was personified in a goddess of the same name.

The Book of the Dead spelled out the belief that after death the soul of the deceased proceeded to a chamber called the Hall of the Two Truths, where wrongdoing in the course of his or her life on Earth was to be denied. Each individual's heart was then weighed in the balance against the feather of truth. A monstrous creature known as Ammit devoured the hearts of those found to have lied, who were subsequently condemned to remain eternally in the Underworld. In contrast those who had spoken truly were admitted to the company of the god Osiris in the fields of Aaru, the Egyptian heaven.

Inanna's knot

One of the few visual symbols to have survived from ancient Mesopotamia, Inanna's knot was the emblem of the Sumerian goddess of sexual love and war, known to successor civilizations as Ishtar. It takes the form of a bundle of reeds with the upper end looped, and is thought to represent a doorpost designed to hold a crosspole; usually two were shown together, one for each side. The design is on the famous Warka Vase, a decorated alabaster container dating back

DJED
This ring-
topped pillar
represented
the backbone
of Osiris and
was a symbol
of strength
and stability. It
took its name
from the city
of Djedu, a cult
centre of the
god.

to at least 3000BCE. Scholars speculate that the doorposts may have represented the portal of a storehouse, signifying plenty.

Labrys

When Greece's authoritarian leader Ioannis Metaxas (1871–1941) needed an icon for the youth movement he founded, he chose the *labrys* – the double-headed axe that remains the most familiar emblem of Minoan Crete. For Metaxas the image represented both antiquity and authority.

FARAVAHAR – THE WINGED DISK

Zoroastrian Persia's best-known contribution to world iconography is the *faravahar*, the image of a human figure superimposed on a winged disk. The individuals depicted were *fravashi*, celestial spirits or guardian angels believed to have assisted the sky lord Ahura Mazda in his work of creation. By the time of the Persian Empire, the images of rulers were sometimes used, notably Darius I, whose army the Greeks defeated at the Battle of Marathon in 490BCE. The *faravahar* itself drew on earlier winged-disk symbols from ancient Egypt, where they were associated with the sun god Ra, and from Assyria, where they served as emblems of royalty. In modern times the emblem has been borrowed by various mystical groups including Rosicrucians, Theosophists and Freemasons.

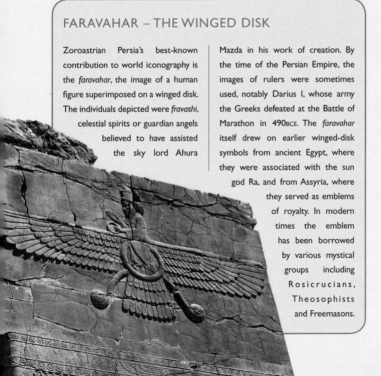

THE CLASSICAL WORLD
Mementoes of the myths

ORPHIC EGG
Orphism used
the serpent-
entwined
egg to signify
the Cosmos.
Clasped in the
coils of a snake,
symbol of
spiritual rebirth
and renewal,
the egg can also
be read as man
emerging from
ignorance once
the shell has
been broken
by initiation
into the Orphic
mysteries.

Even today, the modern Western world remains connected to Classical Greece and Rome by an umbilical cord of shared cultural traditions. Forming part of that heritage is a repertoire of symbols. Often our debt to the ancients goes unrecognized. When superstitious people throw a pinch of spilt salt over their shoulder, they are unlikely to realize the gesture was originally one of respect to the Penates, Roman gods of household plenty; if someone describes an acquaintance as two-faced, they probably do not spare a thought for Janus, the twin-visaged deity of entrances and exits. Yet some of the borrowings have been deliberate. The US Senate still meets in the Capitol, named for Rome's Capitoline Hill, and Mussolini's Fascism took its name and emblem from the *fasces* carried before Roman magistrates.

Orphic egg

The Cosmic Egg from which the universe was hatched is a common mythological theme found in lands as far apart as China, India and pre-Columbian America. In ancient Greece, followers of the Orphic mystery religion believed creation began with an egg (left) laid in the primal Chaos, described as "the womb of darkness". From it emerged Phanes, the hermaphroditic first progenitor of life, from whose offspring the races first of gods and then of humans were born.

Caduceus

Roman heralds traditionally carried a white wand wrapped with ribbons when treating for peace. By a natural process of transference the staff became an emblem of Hermes, messenger of the gods,

THE GORGON'S STONY STARE

In Greek myth the three Gorgons were hideous females with sharp fangs, protruding tongues, bronze claws and snakes for hair. Their faces were so ghastly that all who saw them turned to stone. Greeks sought to harness the lethal power of the image by copying it onto amulets, entrances, city walls and shields – and even tombstones. Known as the *gorgoneion*, the face was thought to ward off malign influences and protect against the Evil Eye.

A *gorgoneion* (1) decorates a bowl made in the 7th century BCE. The frieze around the central image includes two sphinxes (2) and a siren (3).

SIREN
The sirens of
Classical myth
lured seamen
to their deaths
with the
beauty of their
song – hence
their depiction
with avian
attributes. But
over time, the
physical beauty
of a siren has
often been as
relevant – in
many medieval
guises she
appears more
like a mermaid
(above).

acquiring on the way wings like those sported by Hermes himself. More bizarrely, the *caduceus* was shown with twin serpents entwined around it (see opposite), reflecting a story that the god had disturbed two snakes fighting and made peace by thrusting the rod between them. In later times the *caduceus* became a symbol of commerce and communications, reflecting Hermes' role as a speedy courier.

Rod of Asclepius

The *caduceus* has sometimes been confused with the Rod of Asclepius, Greek god of medicine, which takes the form of a staff entwined

FRONDS OF FERTILITY

The palmette decorations favoured in Classical times took their place in a line of motifs drawn from plant life stretching back to the earliest civilizations. Ancient Egyptian artists drew their inspiration from the papyrus reeds found in the Nile Delta or from lotus flowers, whose radiating shape may have influenced the palmette's own design. The Greeks themselves developed the palmette into the more intricate acanthus-leaf pattern, reflecting the fecundity of the natural world. Acanthus remained a popular ornamentation into the 20th century.

The lotus motif (left) preceded the palmette (centre), which itself may have influenced the acanthus design (right).

by a single serpent. Like the Orphic egg, the snake represents healing and regeneration, reflecting the ancient belief that snakes could renew themselves by shedding their skins. Asclepius's staff continues to be an internationally recognized symbol of therapeutic care, featuring today in the logos of the World Health Organization, the American Medical Association and the Royal Army Medical Corps.

Siren

The bird-like sirens of Classical myth lured seamen to their deaths with the beauty of their song. In Homer's *Odyssey*, Ulysses protected his sailors from the sirens' charms by filling their ears with wax; he himself was lashed to the mast so they could not entice him. Symbolically, sirens are temptresses in any form, and the siren song is any message that is as alluring as it is dangerous.

Laurel wreath

The leaves of the Bay laurel had multiple connotations for the ancient Greeks. They were associated with poetry, and were thought to inspire prophecy; the Pythoness at Delphi chewed them to stimulate her oracular powers. They were also linked with immortality, the laurel tree being evergreen. As a result, victors in the Pythian Games, held every four years at Delphi, were rewarded with a wreath of the leaves (winners in the ancient Olympics received an olive branch). The Romans seized on the connection with winning to make the wreath a symbol of victory; news of battles won was sent to the Senate wrapped in laurel leaves, and the successful generals were crowned with laurels to celebrate their triumphs.

PALMETTE
The fan-shaped
leaves of the
palm tree were
a common
architectural
motif from
Classical to
neo-Classical
times (right).
Besides being
aesthetically
appealing,
the palmette
symbolized
fertility and
growth.

Fasces

In July 1943, when news of Mussolini's fall spread in Rome, jubilant crowds started pulling down images of bundles of rods surrounding an axe. The emblem was the logo of his Fascist Party. The Italian dictator had borrowed the idea from the trussed birch staves borne by the *lictors* of ancient Rome (see opposite). Representing strength through unity, the *fasces* has survived its association with Fascism and lives on today across the world as a symbol of governmental authority, featuring, for example, on the official seal of the US Senate.

Cornucopia

The image of a horn overflowing with fruit and vegetables remains a potent international symbol of the Earth's bounty. Greek myth explained that the infant Zeus was fed goat's milk by the nymph Amalthea, and that he rewarded her by breaking off one of the animal's horns and giving it to her with the promise that its owner should always have everything she wanted in abundance.

Omphalos

Across the prehistoric Mediterranean region, people accorded sacred powers to conical stones or boulders, to which the Greeks gave the name *omphalos* ("navel"). The most celebrated example was kept in the sanctuary of Delphi, where it was said to mark the centre of the world. Legend had it that Zeus released two eagles from the far ends of the Earth and placed the stone at the point where they met.

THE POWER OF THE MANY

The *lictors* of ancient Rome were attendant officials who preceded magistrates whenever they went out on public business, clearing a path for them and forming a protective line when they sought to address a crowd. However, perhaps their principal function was to emphasize the dignity of their employers, and every aspect of their appearance was designed to underline that message. They wore the togas of Roman citizens and carried the *fasces*, which symbolized magisterial authority as well as warning of the consequences of transgression: the rods and the axe bound together in a bundle signified respectively corporal and capital punishment.

Besides the *fasces* bundle (1), the *lictor* represented in this bronze Roman figurine carries laurel leaves (2) and wears a wreath (3) – symbols of authority and civilian power.

HINDUISM
Route-markers for dharma

Hinduism is a Western term, used as a catch-all to describe interlinked ancient religious traditions of the Indian subcontinent. Unlike the followers of most other major faiths, Hindus have no set body of beliefs or institutional structure. Instead, different regions have separate traditions with regard to the gods they worship, the scriptures they use and the festivals they observe.

Underlying the diversity are some common concepts. One is *dharma*, which means "justice" and implies the right way of living in accordance with natural moral laws. Most Hindus accept the idea of reincarnation or the transmigration of souls, linked through *samsara*, the cycle of birth and rebirth through successive generations. The law of *karma* dictates that a person's behaviour in one life will determine the conditions of his existence in the next. The ultimate goal is *moksha* or liberation, meaning release from the cycle of death and rebirth.

AUMKAR
Perhaps the most important Hindu symbol, the *aumkar* is the visual representation of "aum" or "om", a deeply resonant sound said to be the noise through which the world was created.

NATARAJA: LORD OF THE DANCE

One of Hinduism's best-known symbols is Shiva as Nataraja, Lord of the Dance. The god is shown engaged in the divine dance of creation and destruction, concentrating within himself all the energies of the universe. The pose achieved its familiar form in bronzes of the Chola kingdom of southern India in the 10th to 12th centuries CE, but it drew on much earlier oriental traditions of sacred dancing, used as a way of reaching an ecstatic state. Nataraja may also appear as an ascetic with matted hair, a conquering warrior, or androgynously, combining his own attributes with those of his partner, the goddess Shakti.

Shiva dances in a flame circle
(1) to represent the universe,
crushing Apasmara (2), who
stands for ignorance. The snake
(3) is Kundalini, physical energy.

The Hindu tradition is polytheistic, accepting many gods. The chief divinities are grouped in a triad known as the Trimurti: Brahma, a remote and unapproachable creator deity, Vishnu and Shiva. These may be worshipped in their own right or else as manifestations of an overriding divine principle, Brahman. They can also take different

KALI YANTRA

Yantras are geometric – or "shape-energy" – diagrams used by Hindus as a focus for meditation. This example is inspired by Kali, the fearsome goddess of creation and destruction. The lotus represents reproductive vital force. The perimeter has four openings to the regions of the universe. The circle is ignorance. The triangle is *shakti* (creative energy); pointing down it represents the *yoni* or female sexuality.

forms: Vishnu, for example, may be venerated as any one of nine different avatars or incarnations, among them such popular figures as Krishna, Rama and the lion-man Narashima.

Besides the Trimurti, other important Hindu deities include the elephant-headed Ganesha (right), the Lord of Success and destroyer of evils and obstacles, and the 10-armed warrior goddess Durga, who embodies feminine creative energy (*shakti*).

Mace

One of four attributes traditionally associated with Vishnu (along with the *chakra*, lotus and conch shell), the mace is a weapon for battling the forces of evil. Esoterically it is interpreted as primal energy.

Chakra

Another of Vishnu's attributes, the *chakra* is a bladed, discus-like weapon that also represents the god's martial side. Spiritually it is seen as the cutting edge that slices through self-delusion to reach true inner vision.

Vel

Different parts of India have their own divinities, and the warrior god Murugan is a favourite in the southern Tamil lands. His emblem is the *vel* or lance, given to him by his mother Parvati to use against demons. The Vel of Murugan is now worshipped in some Tamil temples as a symbol of the victory of good over evil, and Parvati's gift is still celebrated annually in the festival of Thaipusam.

TRISHULA
Shiva's trident,
his cosmic
weapon
as creator,
preserver,
destroyer.
It is also a
fire symbol
representing
three aspects
of the Vedic
god Agni.

Trishula

Shiva's weapon is the *trishula* or trident, often carried by Shaivite *sannyasis* (ascetics). The three-pronged symbol representing it resembles the Buddhist *triratna* (see pages 100–101), which may derive from it. Different schools associate the triple projections with varying trinities: past, present and future in one interpretation; creation, existence and destruction in another.

Nandi

Another of Shiva's attributes is the bull Nandi, which serves as the god's mount and also as the gatekeeper whose statue can be seen outside Shaivite temples. White in colour, the animal stands for purity and justice.

Lingam

Modern Hindu interpretations shy away from identifying the *lingam*, a sacred emblem of Shiva, with the phallus, which it obviously resembles. A very ancient symbol whose origins date back as far as the Indus Valley civilization, the *lingam* may well have begun its career as a sign of masculine potency and strength. Hindu scholars today translate the term simply as "mark" and see it as a visual interpretation of Shiva's power and a focus for worship of the god.

Tilaka

Usually worn on the forehead, the *tilaka* is an identifying mark that serves to signal the particular Hindu tradition that the wearer follows. Various substances are used to make it, including clay, ashes and sandalwood paste. Some people choose to wear the *tilaka* daily, others only for religious ceremonies.

KALKI

Hindu scriptures describe Vishnu as manifesting himself in nine separate incarnations, plus one which is still to come. This future avatar is Kalki, a warrior deity who will appear on Earth to bring to an end the current cycle of existence, the Kali Yuga, an age of darkness and corruption. In this aspect he is usually shown riding a winged white horse and brandishing a sword. Kalki is not worshipped, as Vishnu's other avatars are; instead he is a figure whose coming is linked to the dawn of a new age.

In this 19th-century bronze, Kalki and his steed form a single figure. In his hands the god holds the traditional attributes of Vishnu: conch shell (1), lotus (2), mace (3) and *chakra* wheel (4).

BUDDHISM

Signposts to enlightenment

Founded in about the 5th century BCE by Siddhartha Gautama, Buddhism teaches individuals how to lose themselves in a greater, universal consciousness. Gautama himself became the Buddha, or Enlightened One, at the age of 35 and spent the rest of his life passing on the lessons he had learned to a growing band of disciples. Others since have similarly attained enlightenment, and they too are considered to be *buddhas*.

Gautama summarized his teaching in the Four Noble Truths. These state that the condition of life is suffering; that the root cause of suffering is desire; that overcoming desire puts an end to suffering; and that desire can be vanquished by following the mental and moral disciplines known as the Noble Eightfold Path. The path entails an ethical lifestyle based on right speech, right actions, and right livelihood (one that does not harm others). Mentally it requires contemplation involving right exercise of the mind, right awareness and right meditation. These in turn promote wisdom, represented by right thoughts and right understanding. The ultimate goal is *bodhi* ("awakening"), freeing the individual from the eternal cycle of suffering and leading him or her to *nirvana*, the final extinction of desire.

Dharma wheel

The concept of *dharma* plays a key role in the Buddhist worldview, as in other religions originating on the Indian subcontinent. The word signifies a life lived in harmony with the natural order, and in the Buddhist context also includes the Buddha's own teaching. The

DHARMA WHEEL
The eight spokes of the Buddhist wheel correspond to the right actions of the Eightfold Path. A variation forms part of India's national flag.

THE BUDDHA'S FOOTPRINTS

Images of the Buddha's footprints, known as Buddhapadas, are found across the Buddhist world, but are particularly revered in Sri Lanka and Thailand. Rock markings of human body parts date back to prehistoric times and have a name of their own: petrosomatoglyphs. In India there was a tradition of holy footprints that predated the arrival of Buddhism, symbolizing the passage of the transcendent on Earth. In the Buddhist tradition the prints not only implied the Buddha's physical presence in the material world but also his departure from it into the state of *nirvana*, attained by following the Eightfold Path to enlightenment.

This Buddhapada from the Amaravati Stupa in India features concentric *dharma* wheels (1) on the sole of each foot. Faint incisions on the heels reveal the *triratna* symbol (2), while swirling swastikas (3) appear in the spaces between the wheels and toes.

SWASTIKA
This popular
Buddhist motif
is considered
the seal of the
Buddha's heart.
The symbol is
one of success
and prosperity.

Buddhist symbol of *dharma* is an eight-spoked wheel, each of the spokes representing one element of the Buddha's Noble Eightfold Path. The Buddha himself is said to have turned such a wheel in the first great sermon he preached after attaining enlightenment, delivered at Sarnath near India's border with Nepal. The turning of the wheel symbolizes the process of spiritual change set in motion by his teaching, but also refers to the endless cycle of *samsara*, or rebirth, which can only be escaped by following his precepts.

Triratna

The *dharma* also features as one of the *triratna* or "three jewels" of Buddhism (the other two are the Buddha himself and the Sangha – the monastic community). This trinity is invoked in ordination

THE MEANING OF MUDRAS

Symbolic hand gestures known as *mudras* play an important role in Buddhist art. Adapted from Hindu yoga positions, each one carries a specific connotation. The *dhyana mudra* (left) is the traditional posture of meditation. Recalling the turning of the *dharma* wheel, the *dharmachakra* (centre) refers to the Buddha's first great sermon, preached at Sarnath. The *vitarka mudra* (right), with the tips of thumb and index finger touching, denotes the transmission of Buddhist teachings.

ceremonies, when novices repeat "I take refuge in the Buddha; I take refuge in the Dharma; I take refuge in the Sangha". Usually its symbol is a "W" shape with rounded curves, although it may also be represented as three circles enclosed within a clover-shaped outline. The three jewels symbol often appears in conjunction with other emblems, including the lotus flower (see pages 37–39) and the *vajra* or thunderbolt, to form a propitious cluster.

Treasure vase

Also known as the Urn of Wisdom, the treasure vase represents *shunyata* – "emptiness", or "the void" – implying an awareness of the illusory nature of external appearances. In popular Buddhism the vase has also come to stand for health, prosperity and wisdom.

Stupa

Stupas are Buddhist shrines, originally built to house relics of holy men but later becoming objects of veneration in their own right. Over time their distinctive shape became an emblem of the faith. Traditionally stupas featured a circular dome built on a square base, often with a conical spire on top. The overall look could vary from mound-like to bell-shaped, depending on the dimensions of the various parts. In China and Japan the stupa eventually evolved into the multi-storeyed pagoda.

Buddha's eyes

Stupas with painted eyes gazing to the four directions are a common sight in Nepal. They represent the all-seeing gaze of the Buddha looking

ENDLESS KNOT The Endless Knot, a repeated pattern of interlacing forms, symbolizes the Buddha's infinite wisdom and compassion.

out over all points of the world. A spiral symbol is often added where the eyes join; this is the Nepalese numeral "1", added as a reminder of the unity of all existence and to indicate that the Buddha's teachings are the sole path to enlightenment – itself sometimes symbolized by a third eye positioned above the other two.

Endless Knot

A repeated pattern of intertwining forms, the Endless Knot evokes the complexity and interconnectedness of life, as well as the blending of wisdom and compassion required of those seeking enlightenment.

Enso

Meaning "circle" in Japanese, the *enso* – a brushstroke in the form of a ring – is a calligraphic emblem profoundly linked with Zen Buddhism. The image represents enlightenment and the totality of being, but the spontaneous individuality of the brushmarks – for no two *enso* are exactly the same – also implies the transience of the physical world.

Manji

This Japanese term denotes the Buddhist swastika. With the prongs facing left, the symbol implies love and mercy. Turned to the right, it stands for strength and intelligence. Often the two are set off against one another at the top and bottom of Buddhist scriptures.

Conch shell

A rarity in nature, a conch shell that spirals to the right stands for the deep harmony of the Buddha's teachings, which awakens disciples from the sleep of ignorance and directs them along the Noble Eightfold Path.

THE EIGHT-PETALLED LOTUS

In Buddhism a lotus flower stands for the enlightened soul and is sometimes shown with eight petals – an important number for the faith. Known in the West as water lilies, the plants have their roots in the muddy bottoms of ponds but the flowers bloom on the surface in the sunlight. Buddhism teaches that the human spirit can similarly rise from the mire of the material world through the waters of experience up to the radiance of enlightenment. The Buddha is often shown sitting on a lotus flower.

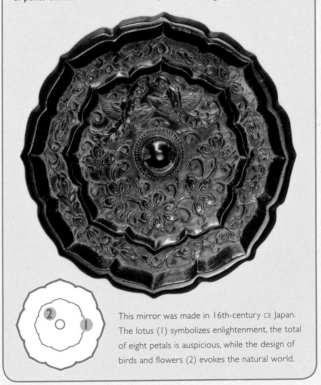

This mirror was made in 16th-century CE Japan. The lotus (1) symbolizes enlightenment, the total of eight petals is auspicious, while the design of birds and flowers (2) evokes the natural world.

JAINISM
Respect for all living things

JAINISM
This universe symbol adopted by all Jain sects incorporates key elements of the faith – the Lok outline, the raised hand, a swastika, the three jewels and the abode of the *siddha*s.

Jainism developed out of, but in opposition to, India's Hindu traditions. It traces its origins to a line of 24 *tirthankar*s – literally "ford-makers" – whose teaching helps individual souls to cross from the bondage of the material world to liberation from the cycle of rebirth. The first of these pioneers may have lived as early as the 9th century BCE; the last, Vardhamana, is generally dated 599–527BCE, and is known as Mahavira ("Great Hero") or Jina ("Victor").

Reacting against Hinduism's caste elitism and the practice of animal sacrifice, Jainism opened itself to all and preached the sanctity of life. In other respects Jains remained close to the earlier tradition, sharing with it the concept of *samsara* (the cycle of reincarnation) and the law of *karma* that dictates people's condition in future lives. Jainism shares symbols with both Hinduism and Buddhism, which developed on the subcontinent at a similar period. Upon the 2,500th anniversary of Mahavira's enlightenment, the Jain sects agreed a general symbol (left). Outlined by Lok – the Jain universe (seven hells at the bottom, Earth and the planets in the middle, the heavenly realms at the top) – it contains the raised hand and the swastika, as well as three dots for the Buddhist-derived idea of three jewels (right knowledge, right faith and right conduct). At the top an arc represents the Siddhashila, the final resting place of those perfected souls that have been liberated. The dot within the arc is a *siddha*, one who is free of attachments.

Swastika

Thousands of years before it was appropriated by the Nazis, the swastika played a prominent part in the iconography of most Indian religions. As the *fylfot* it remains particularly important in Jainism, being associated with the seventh of the faith's 24 *tirthankars* or founding fathers. As such, it appears in all temples and holy books, and celebrants shape swastikas out of rice before altars in the course of rituals. Its four arms remind the faithful of the four destinies in the cycle of death and rebirth: heavenly beings, human beings, animal beings (including birds, insects and plants) and hellish beings. The *fylfot* is also a reminder of the four subdivisions of the Jain Sangh, or community – *sädhus*, *sädhvis*, *shrävaks* and *shrävikäs*.

THE VOW OF AHIMSA

A hand raised in a "stop" sign symbolizes the concept of *ahimsa*, or "avoidance of violence", which Jains interpret to mean not doing harm to any living thing. Because of the belief that the reincarnated soul may come back in animal or insect form, some Jains sometimes wear nose masks to avoid inhaling flies and sweep the path in front of them so as not to tread on bugs.

AHIMSA WITHIN A WHEEL

The *ahimsa* palm symbolizes the Jain vow of non-violence. The wheel represents *samsara*, the eternal cycle of rebirth that Jains hope to escape.

SIKHISM

The khanda, *the* Khalsa *and the five Ks*

KHANDA
A universally recognized symbol of Sikhism, the *khanda* appears on temple flags and even as a finial.

Founded by Guru Nanak (1469–1539) in the Punjab region of northwest India, Sikhism is a monotheistic religion combining elements of Hinduism and Islam. In reaction to the ritualism that marked both those faiths at the time, Nanak sought to bring his followers closer to God through meditation and devotion.

Nanak's message was passed on through a succession of nine later gurus, the last of whom was Gobind Singh, founder of the Khalsa order, which gave the movement a markedly military character. On his death in 1708, Sikh scriptures collected in the *Adi Granth* ("First Book") became the religion's supreme authority. These texts and the entire Sikh community are both now called gurus for their role in passing on the teachings of the founding fathers.

Ek Onkar

Derived from the Hindu *aumkar* sign, the Ek Onkar symbol is a fundamental emblem of Sikhism, made up of the Sanskrit characters for "One Aum" or "One God". Found in most Sikh places of worship, it summarizes the monotheistic nature of the faith.

Khanda

Made up of a collection of weapons, the *khanda* is recognized around the world as a Sikh icon. The *khanda* itself is the double-edged sword in the centre, backed by a sharp-bladed throwing ring (*chakra*) and flanked by single-edged scimitars. Together they convey the warrior image Gobind Singh gave to the faith. The right edge is said to symbolize freedom governed by moral values; the left, divine justice.

THE KHALSA

Sikhism developed at a time when much of northern India fell under the control of the Muslim Mughal Dynasty. Faced with oppression at the hands of the militant Emperor Aurangzeb, Gobind Singh fought back by founding the Khalsa (literally "Pure"), a community open to all who underwent the Sikh initiation ceremony. The Khalsa was initially a warrior brotherhood, and those who joined were expected to practise arms and to be willing to die for their beliefs. It survives to this day as a bulwark of the faith, now open to both men and women.

Sikhs have five articles of faith known as *kakar*s: *kesh* (unshorn hair and beard); *kanga*, a small comb to comb the hair twice daily); *kaccha*, undershorts worn as a symbol of sexual restraint; *kara*, an iron bracelet representing the bond to the Sikh faith; and the *kirpan*, a curved sword or dagger carried for defence. This *kirpan* sword is decorated with the *khanda* motif (1), an image of Gobind Singh (2) and an eagle's head (3) to symbolize valour.

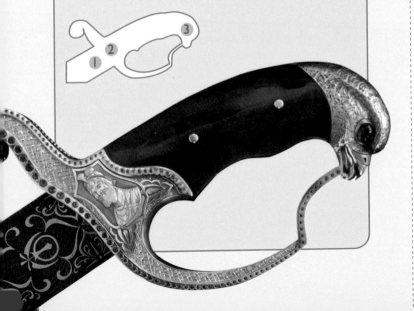

CONFUCIANISM AND TAOISM

Ideograms of Chinese thought

YIN-YANG
The Diagram
of the Supreme
Ultimate
represents
duality as the
dynamic force
in the Cosmos.

Confucianism and Taoism are twin poles of traditional Chinese thought. The two are opposite but complementary in their message. Based on the thoughts of the sage Kongfuzi (Confucius), Confucianism preaches civic virtue, stressing respect for tradition and for elders along with an acceptance of social hierarchies – an apt doctrine for a populous, tightly governed nation. Taoism, whose fundamental text is the *Tao Te Ching* (roughly translated as *The Way and its Power*), in contrast emphasizes spontaneity and the need to live in harmony with nature. Both doctrines emerged in the 6th century BCE, and between them they dominated Chinese intellectual life for the next two and a half millennia. The two came to share an overlapping symbolism that in later centuries also profoundly influenced the iconography of Chinese Buddhism.

Taijitu

Better known in the West as the *yin-yang* symbol, the *taijitu* encapsulates fundamental principles of Taoist thought. The outer circle represents the universe. The two joined shapes are respectively *yin* and *yang*, opposite but complementary forces that constantly interact with one another to shape the cycle of life. *Yin* is passive, dark, female and nocturnal; *yang* is active, light, male and associated with the day. The image of the world they convey is one of dynamic balance; the two fluctuating impulses are constantly in motion, one advancing as the other retreats – as manifested in such antitheses as shadow and sun, intuition and reason, and non-being and being.

TRIGRAMS FOR A WORLD IN FLUX

Trigrams are arrangements of three lines stacked horizontally above one another. They form the basic unit of the *I Ching* or *Book of Changes*, an ancient text and one of Confucianism's Five Classics. A line is either broken (*yin*) or unbroken (*yang*), making eight combinations. Trigrams are in turn combined, one above another, to form hexagrams, each composed of two trigrams or six *yin* or *yang* lines, raising the number of possibilities for oracular purposes to 64. Each hexagram represents a particular state or process. The sequence below shows, in the outer circle, the Primal Arrangement of opposites (fire and water), and, in the interior circle, the Inner World Arrangement or seasonal cycle.

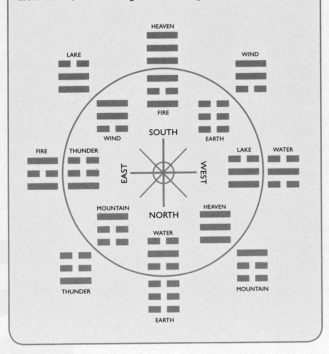

THE BAGUA

Having their roots in divination as practised by soothsayers advising early Chinese kings, trigrams eventually acquired a symbolic power of their own as representations of the physical universe. Each one is identified with a given compass direction and also with a natural phenomenon: earth, air, fire, water, mountain, lake, wind and thunder. Together they form an image of the physical world that finds emblematic expression in the *bagua* – a circular arrangement of the eight trigrams with the *yin-yang* symbol of cosmic dualities in its centre. The *bagua* is an important emblem in *fengshui*, thought to favour the flow of *qi*, the life-force.

A protective amulet shows a tiger (1) – an auspicious image of power – beneath a *bagua* (2). In the centre of the circle the *yin-yang* symbol (3) represents the principle of transience also implicit in the trigrams, which reflect a world in a state of constant flux – the changes spelled out in the divinatory *I Ching* or *Book of Changes*.

Qilin

A propitious beast of legend, the qilin only appears in the lifetimes of outstanding individuals of exceptional virtue – in practice, usually celebrated emperors. Sometimes called the Chinese unicorn, it has a single horn on its head, along with the body of a deer, the hooves of a horse and the tail of an ox. The qilin is a sign of good times, and people count themselves fortunate to be born when one is sighted.

Clouds

Known as *yun*, clouds represent the celestial realm and stylized cloud spirals (right) symbolize happiness and good luck, hence their inclusion as part of the design of the Olympic Torch for the games in Beijing in 2008.

Si Xiang

Literally meaning "Four Symbols", this term covered four mythological creatures identified in traditional Chinese astronomy with different groups of constellations. Each one was also linked to a season and a point of the compass. The azure dragon, one of many auspicious dragons to populate Chinese folklore, was associated with springtime and the east. The vermilion bird represented summer and the south, and because of its reddish-orange hue was also linked to fire. The white tiger, standing for autumn and the west, was also connected with great age, for Chinese folklore maintained that tigers grew white as they got older. The beast that was emblematic of winter and the north was the black tortoise, which also had connotations of long life, as tortoises generally symbolized longevity.

SHINTOISM

Japan's way of the spirits

TOMOE
The tadpole-
shaped *tomoe*
symbol is
often shown
(as above) in
triplicate within
a circle to form
a *mitsu tomoe*.
Associated
with the war
god Hachiman,
it was adopted
as a samurai
emblem.

The traditional religion of Japan, Shinto is an animist faith dedicated to the propitiation of *kami*, or spirits. Sometimes these are localized guardian beings, but others are more like gods, linked with particular phenomena (such as storms) or with activities (for instance, agriculture and industry). One line of *kami* tracing its descent from the sun goddess Amaterasu was traditionally viewed as the progenitors of Japan's imperial family.

Leading *kami* are worshipped at shrines, well over 100,000 of which are in operation around Japan today. In addition, many families have small household altars. From 1868 to 1945 a form of state Shintoism was promoted by the government as a way of fostering national unity and emperor worship. The nationalist affiliations of the movement left it discredited after World War II, however, when the emperor in a radio broadcast publicly disclaimed his divine lineage. Today Shinto's "Four Attributes" are said to be respect for the family, including ancestors; a feeling for nature; cleanliness, which has ritual significance; and attendance of Shinto festivals.

Turtle

A symbol of good fortune and longevity, the turtle was generally a propitious omen in Japanese tradition. Known as *genbu*, it drew many of its symbolic associations from China, where the Black Tortoise was one of the Four Symbols representing constellations in traditional Chinese astronomy, associated with winter and the north (see page 111). It also served as an

DECORATED TSUBA

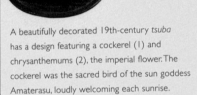

Tsuba were ornamental guards that protected the hands of people wielding Japanese swords. Over the centuries they came to be richly decorated, providing miniature canvases for the depiction of symbols. Emblems of strength and courage were popular, and samurai often chose to adorn the hilts of favourite weapons with the family crests known as *mon*. Generations of craftsmen dedicated themselves to producing the guards, with distinctive styles and traditions.

A beautifully decorated 19th-century *tsuba* has a design featuring a cockerel (1) and chrysanthemums (2), the imperial flower. The cockerel was the sacred bird of the sun goddess Amaterasu, loudly welcoming each sunrise.

image of the universe, its domed shell representing the sky while its body stood for the Earth. In Japan the turtle became an emblem of strength and endurance, often conceived as an indomitable warrior.

Chrysanthemum

The chrysanthemum is the emblem of the Japanese imperial family, whose seal is a stylized yellow or orange flower with 16 petals radiating from a central circle. White chrysanthemums are associated with death; they are worn at funerals and used as grave decorations.

JUDAISM

God's covenant with His chosen people

STAR OF DAVID
This six-pointed star is the most widely recognized symbol of the Jewish faith, although its use dates back only to the Middle Ages. Today it also represents the state of Israel, appearing on the national flag.

Judaism is the religion of the Jewish people, based on a covenant between God and the patriarch Abraham. It is a monotheistic faith, affirming the existence of a single, omniscient deity. Its principal source of authority is the Hebrew Bible, which spells out the history of the special relationship forged between God and the Jews during the course of the 2nd and 1st millennia BCE. The divine instructions for the right ordering of society are spelled out in the Torah ("law"), preserved in the Talmud. Over the past century or so, different interpretations of the Judaic heritage have coalesced in two parallel traditions, Conservative and Reform Judaism, both of which have in turn bred splinter groups. Judaism does not actively seek to proselytize, but accepts "righteous converts" who sincerely accept the faith.

Tetragrammaton

Greek for "four-letter word", the tetragrammaton is the name given to a sequence of four Hebrew letters

representing the name of the God of Israel. Once transliterated into English as JHVH ("Jehovah"), the tetragrammaton now more often appears as YHWH ("Yahweh"). Judaism forbids the pronunciation of the name outside of the Temple in Jerusalem, so believers make do with euphemisms such as *hashem* ("the name"). Those who transgress risk taking the name of the Lord in vain – an action that some Jewish traditions considered enough to prevent a soul from entering Heaven.

THE SANCTUARY VESSELS

In late 13th-century Spain there developed a rabbinical iconographic tradition that involved adorning the preliminary folios of Hebrew Bibles with the cult objects believed to have been in the Temple of Solomon. One of the earliest surviving examples (below) of this art is from Aragon, dates from 1299 and is believed to be the work of Solomon ben Raphael. Bordering the picture are passages from Numbers 8:4 and Exodus 25:34 that describe a lampstand (*menorah*) and cups. Divided into four sections, the panels of the artwork each contain objects described in Exodus and Numbers (as well as Deuteronomy for the Ten Commandments). The arrangement of the loaves, the pans of frankincense above them and the decorative elements of the lampstand all conform to descriptions in the eighth book of the *Mishneh Torah* by Jewish philosopher Maimonides.

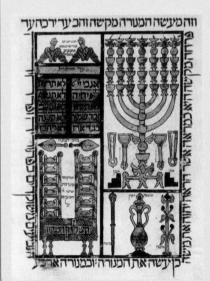

The *menorah* and its tongs and snuffers (1); the jar of *manna* flanked by the rods of Aaron (2); the cherubim seated on the ark cover (3); and the showbreads and tablets of the Ten Commandments (4).

CHAI
Consisting of the Hebrew letters *het* and *yod*, the word *chai* means "life". In Jewish numerology the letters add up to 18, a lucky number for Jews, who often give gifts of money in multiples of 18. The symbol is popular as a necklace adornment.

Ten Commandments

The number 10 has special significance in Judaism because of its link to the Ten Commandments given to Moses by God on Mt. Sinai. The number signifies completeness.

Pomegranate

A propitious fruit in Jewish tradition, the pomegranate is associated with righteousness because it supposedly has 613 seeds, corresponding to the 613 *mitzvot*, or commandments of the Torah. The Book of Exodus specified that images of the fruit should be woven onto priestly robes. Many Jews still eat pomegranates at Rosh Hashanah, the Jewish New Year festival.

RECEPTACLES FOR GOD'S WORD

The Book of Deuteronomy prescribes that the faithful should inscribe a short prayer (Shema Yisrael) commencing "Hear, O Israel: The Lord our God is one Lord …" on the gates and doorposts of their houses. Known as the *mezuzah*, the document is still displayed by observant Jews. The parchments containing the words are usually contained in symbolically decorated cases (right), whose material and imagery varies widely.

Made in Renaissance Italy, this polished bone *mezuzah* is adorned with several symbols. The letters at the top of the case, and visible on the parchment, spell *shaddai* ("Almighty").

Lion of Judah

Associated everywhere with strength and courage, the lion in Jewish tradition is specifically the emblem of the house of Judah, the most influential of the 12 tribes. The Lion of Judah was subsequently adopted as the symbol of the Ethiopian royal family, who traced their origins to a son of the union between King Solomon and the Queen of Sheba. It is used today as an emblem (right) of the city of Jerusalem.

Lulav

A frond of the date palm tree, the *lulav* is one of the Four Species – the others are the myrtle, willow and citron fruit – featured in daily prayer services during the festival of Sukkot, as instructed in the Book of Leviticus. The four symbolize agricultural fertility. Like pomegranates, date palms are also associated with upright behaviour.

Menorah

A fundamental icon of the faith, the *menorah* or seven-branched candlestick traces its origins to the candelabrum used first in the Tabernacle, then in the Temple in Jerusalem. The Book of Exodus describes the construction of the original, which was beaten from a single piece of gold. The *menorah* was part of the spoils seized after the fall of Jerusalem in 70CE, as depicted on the Arch of Titus in Rome. A symbol of spiritual illumination, its seven branches have been variously associated with the days of the week or the seven heavenly planets known to antiquity.

CHRISTIANITY

Mysteries of the Trinity and the Passion

In its early centuries, Christianity defined itself by its symbols. The cross in particular enjoyed a triumphal progress around the globe, making its stark form one of the world's most widely recognized emblems. The symbols of Christianity are now so ubiquitous that it is easy to forget their origins as a private code. Yet for the first three

THREE FISH
The Christian triune God or Trinity has many symbols, with one of the oldest and most popular being three entwined fish or a fish with three heads.

SACRED MONOGRAMS

From the early Christian era references to Jesus have been abbreviated into sacred monograms. These include the *chi rho* (see opposite), IHC or IHS ("Jesus") and INRI ("Jesus of Nazareth, King of the Jews"). The ornate decoration on the 6th-century sarcophagus (below) of Archbishop Theodore in Ravenna includes the Chi Rho with the letters Alpha and Omega, signifying that Jesus is the beginning and the end.

The dove (1), peacock (2) and vines (3) appear with the Alpha and Omega and *chi rho* monogram (4) on this sarcophagus in Ravenna.

centuries of its history, Christianity was a proscribed faith whose adherents often had to worship in secret. In the years of persecution, the Church relied on signs as one way of communicating with the faithful. The markings were clandestine statements of belief, a secret language only initiates understood.

Ichthys

One of the earliest secret symbols used by Christians was the fish, which has been found in the form of graffiti from the 1st century CE on. The mark drew its significance from a pun: in Greek, the five characters that made up the word *ichthys*, or "fish", also formed an acronym for the phrase "Jesus Christ Son of God, Saviour". Christians also no doubt bore in mind Jesus' words to the Apostles: "I will make you fishers of men".

The earliest surviving written reference to the fish symbol comes from Clement of Alexandria, in around 200CE. Clement recommended that Christians should feature fish or dove motifs on their personal seals, the dove being an image of the Holy Spirit. Shortly afterwards Clement's contemporary Tertullian, based in Carthage, spelled out the play on words in an essay on baptism: "We, little fishes, after the example of our *ichthys* Jesus Christ, are born in water".

Chi rho

Another image that had huge importance in the spread of Christianity was the *chi rho* sign, made up of the Greek characters representing "ch" and "r" – the first two letters of Christ's name. Visually the *chi* symbol resembles an "x", while *rho* looks like an elongated "p". Linked together, they formed a monogram that stood not just for Jesus himself but also for his Church.

CHI RHO
This Christian
monogram was
popularized
by Emperor
Constantine.

First recorded on Christian tombs in the 3rd century CE, the symbol rose to prominence when it was adopted by the Roman Emperor Constantine, the first to extend toleration to his Christian subjects. Contemporary accounts claimed that on the eve of a crucial battle he dreamed he saw the image in the sky and heard the words, "Under this sign you will conquer". He subsequently had the symbol engraved on his soldiers' shields and on his own imperial banner, which became known as the *labarum*. Constantine went on to win a crushing victory, defeating a rival claimant to the imperial throne, and subsequently himself converted to Christianity.

Cross

The most profound, enduring and universal of all Christian symbols, the cross comes in many different forms. The classic cross has a vertical bar longer than the horizontal, whereas a Greek cross has arms of equal length. A cross rotated 45 degrees to form an "X" shape is known as a saltire or St Andrew's cross. The Eastern Orthodox cross has a short bar above the horizontal arm, said to represent the headboard used in the Crucifixion, and a slanting lower rib, popularly thought to indicate a footrest partly dislodged by Christ in his death-throes. The upside-down St Peter's cross, with the transverse spar at the bottom, is now generally associated with Satanism, reflecting a deliberate rejection of the Christian tradition.

DOVE
This traditional
symbol of
peace also
represents the
Holy Spirit,
which was
said to have
descended on
Jesus after his
baptism "like
a dove".

Pelican

In the Middle Ages pelicans were commonly believed to peck their own breast to feed their young on their blood. As an image of self-sacrifice, the bird subsequently became associated with Jesus, who was thought to have given his life for the good of humankind.

RUSHTON TRIANGULAR LODGE

In Protestant England in the 1590s Roman Catholic nobleman Sir Thomas Tresham built a gamekeeper's lodge on his estates in Northamptonshire. The design was born of the meditations that had occupied him during years spent in prison for his beliefs. In every detail of its groundplan and execution the lodge was intended to reflect the mysteries of the Holy Trinity of Father, Son and Holy Ghost. The lodge is not just triangular in shape, it also has three storeys and a three-sided chimney. Each wall is 33ft (10m) long, inset with three ornate windows, some of them trefoils, some trefoils with triangles, and others of a lozenge design. Crowning the building are nine steep triangular gables with three-sided obelisks.

The central design carved high on each façade features three triangles (1) inside a trefoil (2) – the crest of the Tresham family. By combining this personal emblem with repeated symbols of the Trinity, the lodge's builder was making an individual profession of loyalty to his faith.

Lamb

The connotation of Jesus as sacrificial victim is even more explicit in the symbol of the Agnus Dei or Lamb of God. According to St John's Gospel, John the Baptist, on seeing the young Jesus approaching, said, "Behold the Lamb of God, who takes away the sin of the world". The reference was to the sacrificial lamb offered up at the time of the Passover in ancient Jewish temple sacrifices – itself a reminder of the Paschal Lamb killed on the eve of the Exodus, whose blood on Israelite doorposts diverted the angel of death to Egyptian neighbours instead.

THE ALCESTER TAU CROZIER

A crozier is a church official's staff, based on a shepherd's crook. This ornate 11th-century Anglo-Saxon example shows Christ crucified on one side, while the other (below) reveals Christ risen in triumph (centre), and trampling a lion and dragon, representing sin and death. It is known as a *Tau* crozier after the Greek letter T, referring to its shape.

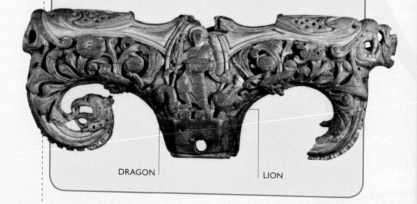

DRAGON

LION

Shepherd

St John's Gospel recorded Jesus telling his followers: "I am the good shepherd, who lays down his life for his sheep". This image too was popular from early times, appearing on the walls of the Roman catacombs from the 1st century on. In later years it transferred easily from Christ himself to the ministers of his Church, seen as tending to the needs of their congregations much as shepherds look after their flocks.

Crozier

A long-established symbol of ecclesiastical authority, the crook-like crozier drew on the Good Shepherd imagery of the early Church. Symbolically its purpose was similar, the curved head being theoretically used to catch the souls of sinners straying from the faith.

Sacred heart

Originating in the Middle Ages, the image of the sacred heart of Jesus is now venerated as an emblem of divine love, primarily in the Roman Catholic Church. The cult became widespread from the 17th century on, when a French nun, St Marguerite Marie Alacoque, experienced a series of visions, in one of which Christ himself authorized her to rest her head upon his heart.

Variations of Christian heart symbolism are numerous. A heart pierced by an arrow represents penitence (this was an emblem of Augustine), whereas a heart pierced by a sword (see above) denotes the Sacred Heart of Mary, a symbol of Mary's love for Jesus and God. A flaming heart conveys the zeal of the true believer. A heart crowned with thorns is an emblem of Ignatius Loyola.

ISLAM

In praise of Allah's name

ALLAH
The name of
God is one
of the most
iconic words
in Arabic
calligraphy.

Meaning "submission" to the will of God, Islam developed out of the teachings of the Prophet Muhammad, who lived in Arabia in the 7th century CE. The teachings are set forth in the Koran, the Muslim holy book. Islam recognizes the divine mission of earlier prophets, including Moses and Jesus, but claims that Muhammad's message superseded theirs, representing the ultimate revelation of God's Word.

Muslims accept five essential props of their religion, known collectively as the Pillars of Islam. One is the profession of faith called the *shahadah* (see below). Another is to pray five times a day at fixed hours, facing in the direction of the holy city of Mecca. The third is the *haj* or pilgrimage to Mecca, to be performed at least once in a lifetime. Then there is the requirement to fast during the month of Ramadan, and finally a duty of alms-giving through the payment of *zakah*, currently interpreted as a 2.5 percent annual levy on savings. Unlike the Christian Church, Islam has no organized hierarchy of priests, but instead accords great respect to scholars and teachers of the faith such as *mullah*s and *ayatollah*s.

**STAR
AND
CRESCENT**
These ancient
celestial
symbols are
universally
identified today
with Islam.

Since its early days, the Islamic community has been split between a majority of Sunni and a minority of Shia, the two parties differing over the line of descent from the Prophet. Islam has also spawned a number of mystical offshoots, the most notable being the Sufi movement.

Islamic law, known as the Sharia, forbids the worship of graven images. At times this prohibition has been interpreted so as to justify a ban on all figurative art. As a result, Islam is short on representational symbols, often preferring calligrams or abstract designs.

THE EIGHT-POINTED STAR

In Islamic art the eight-pointed star was used as a decorative element in its own right and as a repeated background. Sometimes the star shape was elaborated into the pattern known as a *shamsa* ("sun"), with the points as rays radiating from a central circle.

Two overlapping squares, one rotated at a 45-degree angle, form two eight-pointed stars (1, 2) in this Ottoman tile. A circle (3) and an octagon (4) emphasize the mathematical structure underlying creation.

SYMMETRY
The effect of symmetrical patterning in Islamic art, using geometric principles, is, like God, powerful and unifying. This Iranian bowl uses fish to achieve this impression, which is found repeatedly in Islamic decor.

Allah's name

One of the most ubiquitous icons of Islam is the Arabic calligraphic symbol representing Allah's name. Invoking the holy name is in itself a religious act, and over the centuries much skill and ingenuity has been devoted to reproducing it in the most beautiful possible way.

Shahadah

Almost equally familiar are calligraphic representations of the *shahadah*, the creed to which all Muslims subscribe. This twofold profession proclaims that "There is no God but Allah, and Muhammad is his Prophet". The phrase features in the *muezzin*'s daily call to prayer as well as in the prayers themselves, and is also recited by believers at the moment of death.

HAMSA

Sometimes known as the Hand of Fatima in reference to Muhammad's daughter Fatima Zahra, the *hamsa* is an ancient protective talisman guarding the wearer against the Evil Eye. The symbol is particularly popular in North Africa, where it can be seen painted on doors to keep malign influences out of the home. Archaeologists believe that the sign actually predates Islam, perhaps having its origins in the cult of the ancient Carthaginian goddess Tanit. Some Muslims disapprove of its use, regarding it as a vestige of idolatory.

As an icon, the *shahadah* appears on the national flags of Saudi Arabia and Afghanistan, and also on the banner of Al-Qaeda.

Star and crescent

The star and crescent symbol has become closely associated with Islam, and appears on the flags of several Muslim countries, including Malaysia, Turkey and Pakistan. Yet it has no Koranic authority, instead dating from the time of the Ottoman sultans, who adopted it as their insignia. As Ottoman rule spread across the Middle East, so the emblem travelled with them, gaining some religious sanction from the rulers' position as caliphs – temporal and spiritual leaders of the Islamic world.

Enneagram

This nine-pointed star polygon is reputed to be a sign of the presence of God, according to the Naqshbandi Sufi traditions of Central Asia, in which it may have served as a form of numerological divination. The Sufis have saints ("*wali*") but these are not holy people in the Christian sense of that word, but rather people attuned to "reality". Sufis believe that a "design" (*naqsh*) is hidden underneath appearances, which are a falsity: reality – or the true self in the case of individuals – lies beneath. A person must see through outward appearances to discover the truth, the "reality", within; only when they know their real selves can they know "reality". To know this "reality", and then to be able to act on it, is the ultimate goal of Sufism. The enneagram (above, right) is used in New Age personality typology to reveal true motivations and intentions.

BAHA'ISM

Benchmarks for a global faith

NINE-POINTED STAR
Nine has a holy significance in Baha'i, for under the Abjadi system the 28 letters of the Arabic alphabet are given numerical values, and the characters making up the word *baha* ("glory") add up to nine.

The Baha'i faith grew in the 1860s out of an earlier Persian religion, Babism, with its roots in Shia Islam. The name Bab meant "The Gate". When the sect seceded from the Muslim community its followers were persecuted, and the Bab himself was executed in 1850. Before his death he predicted the coming of a new prophet, and in 1863 one of his adherents proclaimed himself to be that chosen one. Taking the name Bahaullah, literally "Glory of God", he claimed a place in a line of divine messengers stretching back through Muhammad, Jesus and the Buddha to Zoroaster and Moses.

Baha'is view all the world's major religions as different approaches to the worship of a single god. Key beliefs include the unity of humankind, equality between peoples and genders, and universal education. They also espouse the idea of an auxiliary language to unite people of all races. Meanwhile, symbols go some way to providing a common idiom that crosses national barriers.

Haykal

RINGSTONE
The two five-pointed stars of the ringstone represent Bab and Bahaullah, the prophets of the present age.

Baha'i inherited from Babism a five-pointed star known as the *haykal*, (literally "temple"). Bahaullah produced many of his writings in the shape of a *haykal*. More common today, though, is a nine-pointed star (see left). The star emblem suggests completion or perfection, while its radiating points reach out like compass directions to all parts of the world. For similar reasons, Baha'i temples often have nine sides, and in Abjad numerology, which attaches numerical values to letters and words in the Arabic alphabet, the numerical value of Baha'i is nine, confirming the faith's unity and perfection.

Ringstone

Baha'is who wish to carry a permanent token of their faith typically do so by bearing the ringstone motif (opposite) of three horizontal bars crossed by a vertical line, flanked on each side by a five-pointed star. The bars represent the worlds of God, of his manifestations, and of humankind; the line running through them stands for the teachings of his messengers, which link the divine and human spheres.

THE DOOR OF THREE LEVELS

The door to the shrine of the Bab, on Mount Carmel, Haifa, Israel (a site chosen by Bahaullah), is laden with symbolism. The design's three horizontal levels represent the worlds of God, His Manifestations (or messengers) and man. As in the ringstone (see above), the vertical line joins the three horizontal bars together, symbolizing the way that the Divine Messengers of God form the link between God and man.

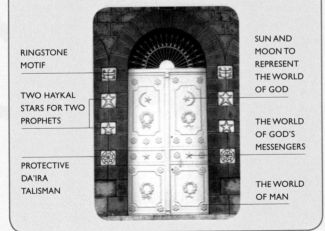

RINGSTONE MOTIF

TWO HAYKAL STARS FOR TWO PROPHETS

PROTECTIVE DA'IRA TALISMAN

SUN AND MOON TO REPRESENT THE WORLD OF GOD

THE WORLD OF GOD'S MESSENGERS

THE WORLD OF MAN

CROSSED CIRCLE
The cross within a circle was an emblem of the Cathars, a medieval group that inherited certain Gnostic beliefs.

ANGUIPEDE
A manifestation of the Gnostic demiurge (see right), this composite creature had the head of a cockerel, the body of a man and snakes for legs.

GNOSTICS AND CATHARS
Guardians of the secret knowledge

In the intellectual cauldron of the late Classical world, a group of thinkers influenced by Judaic and Christian beliefs came together in the conviction that salvation could be achieved through esoteric knowledge. These were the Gnostics (from *gnosis*, Greek for "knowledge"), and for a time in the 2nd century CE their syncretist views represented a real challenge to Christianity. Gnostics were dualists who saw a gulf separating the divine spark in the human mind from the material universe around it. They could not believe that a good, all-powerful God had created the terrestrial world. Instead, they thought it was the work of a corrupted demiurge that they called Ialdabaoth or Iao, identifying it with Jehovah, the vengeful and imperfect deity of the Old Testament. Christ was for them a saving spirit sent from the highest heaven that had inhabited the body of a fallible human called Jesus, deserting it at the time of the Crucifixion. The Gnostics' task was to reintegrate the human spirit with its divine counterpart through revelation of the truth.

Always oriented to an intellectual elite, Gnosticism was largely displaced by orthodox Christianity from the 3rd century on. Yet its ideas lingered, reinforced by the views of an Iranian prophet named Mani. Drawing on ancient Zoroastrian notions, Mani saw the world as a battleground between rival forces of good and evil, both equally powerful. The Manichaean worldview survived Mani's martyrdom in about 276CE and resurfaced in western Europe in the 12th and 13th centuries in the form of Catharism. Like Gnostics before them, Cathars believed that the material world was evil and, like Mani, that Satan was a primordial principle of

THE HOLY GRAIL

Cathars and Gnostics both venerated Christ as a spiritual being sent down from the highest heaven to lead humankind to enlightenment. They viewed Jesus of Nazareth merely as the human vehicle in which the Christ spirit was implanted. In Grail legends, which took shape at the time of the assault on the Cathars, the holy cup – said to contain the blood of Jesus collected by Joseph of Arimathea – came to represent the source of salvation through mystic communion with Christ, while the quest for the receptacle, which some have since claimed the Cathars possessed, was a search for God's grace.

A Ravenna tomb shows a dove (1), representing the Holy Spirit, descending onto a cross (2) in a chalice (3). Grail legends developed at a time when the Church was seeking to relaunch the Eucharistic sacrifice or Mass as a mystical communion.

OCCITAN CROSS
Also known as the Cross of Toulouse, this was the symbol of southwest France's Languedoc region, where the Cathars became most firmly entrenched in the Middle Ages.

evil rivalling the good God. Their goal was to free the spirit from dependence on the material world and restore it to communion with the divine. Catharism attracted followers in much of northern Italy and southern France before it was suppressed on papal orders by the soldiers of the Albigensian Crusade between 1209 and 1229.

Abraxas

According to the Christian writer Tertullian, one Gnostic school taught that the supreme deity was named Abraxas, a name whose characters, according to the then-popular numerological code, totalled 365. Abraxas created 365 separate heavens, each successive one modelled on but slightly inferior to the one above. The lowest was the realm of Jehovah, the God of the Old Testament, seen not as an all-powerful deity but rather as a corrupted angel. In this view Christ was sent not by Jehovah but rather by Abraxas, returning to his realm at the time of the Crucifixion.

The name is also found in Gnostic texts such as the Gospel of the Egyptians. It may represent God and Satan in one entity, a concept in keeping with the duality of the Gnostic worldview. In Thomas More's novel *Utopia*, the island that gives the book its title had the earlier name of Abraxa.

ABRACADABRA
ABRACADABR
ABRACADAB
ABRACADA
ABRACAD
ABRACA
ABRAC
ABRA
ABR
AB
A

Abracadabra

Familiar today as a conjuror's incantation, the word "abracadabra" has a long pedigree dating back to at least the 2nd century CE, when it was written on parchment and used as a charm to cure fevers. One theory of its origin traces it to the Gnostic god Abraxas; another links it to the Aramaic term *abhadda kedhabhra*, meaning "Disappear like this word" – in reference to the diminishing calligramatic form in which it was written (see image, opposite).

Lion Serpent

The *chnoubis* or serpent with the head of a lion was an image inscribed on amulets in the 2nd century CE. It is thought to represent the Gnostic demiurge Ialdabaoth, with the lion's head representing what was left in him of the divine nature and the serpent standing for the part corrupted by contact with the material world.

Alpha and Omega

"I am Alpha and Omega, the first and the last", said God in the Book of Revelation, a reference to the first and last characters in the Greek alphabet. Some Gnostics used the symbols to indicate the totality of the divine creation; others associated it with Ialdabaoth, the demiurge responsible for the creation of the material world.

Holy Grail

Vessels that served as miraculous providers were found in more than one of the world's folklore traditions. Celtic myth had several such, including a cauldron of rebirth that restored dead warriors to life. Such imagery may have fed through into the legend of the Holy Grail, said to be the dish or cup used by Christ at the Last Supper. The legend of the Grail was taking shape at the time of the persecution of the Cathars, and would certainly have been known to them.

KNIGHTS HOSPITALLER AND TEMPLAR

Brethren of the cross and sword

BEAUSÉANT
The Templars
fought beneath
a black-and-
white banner
known as the
Beauséant.
In battle 10
knights were
assigned to
guard the
standard, and
as long as
it was flying
aloft none was
allowed to quit
the field of
combat.

The knightly orders grew up in response to the establishment of the crusader state of Outremer in the Holy Land in the early Middle Ages. The first to be founded was the Order of the Hospital of St John of Jerusalem, or the Hospitallers, based in the institution of that name and at first dedicated to treating the sick. The Templars followed in 1119, taking their name from their home in a building adjoining the supposed site of Solomon's Temple. Their original mission was to protect pilgrims arriving in the Holy Land from Muslim marauders. Both orders flourished thanks to donations and legacies from pious Christians across Europe. The knights followed rules that were part religious and part military. So Templars were forbidden any contact with women – even family members – and had to eat their communal meals in silence; meat was served only three times a week. They also swore absolute allegiance to their superiors in the order.

When Outremer was lost in the late 13th century, the knights had to find a new purpose. The Hospitallers relocated first to Cyprus and then to the Mediterranean island of Rhodes, which they ruled as an independent power. When Rhodes in turn fell to the Ottoman Turks in 1522, they moved again to Malta, which they held until Napoleon finally dislodged them in 1798.

The Templars had a shorter and more violent history. Over the years they acquired strongholds all over Europe and came to act as bankers for rulers and noblemen across the continent. Coveting their wealth, King Philip the Fair of France accused them of heresy and immorality, and tortured confessions out of some of the knights. The order was suppressed by papal decree in 1312, and two years later its last Grand Master, Jacques de Molay, was burned at the stake.

The Templars' brutal end has inspired much speculation. A recent theory proposed that some French Templars sought refuge in Scotland after the suppression of the order, finding shelter there with stonemasons and thereby creating a link between the knights' medieval concept of chivalry and the later development of Freemasonry.

THE MYSTERIOUS CARVINGS OF ROSSLYN

Rosslyn Chapel near Edinburgh is one of Britain's most symbol-rich buildings. Commissioned by William St Clair, Lord Chancellor of Scotland, and built between 1456 and 1486, it contains a mass of carvings apparently tracking the passage of time and the seasons of the year from east to west along its length. It also includes a motif similar to the Templar seal (see page 136). Some researchers have even claimed that a Templar's treasure might lie in a lost vault under the building, although attempts to suggest a closer link with the knights have foundered on the fact that the order was suppressed 150 years before the chapel was built.

This carving of a Green Man (top) – a symbol of untamed nature found in many parts of the world – is one of 110 variations on the theme in and around the chapel. The boss below shows Lucifer as a fallen angel.

Templar cross

The Templars' distinctive insignia was a red cross, typically in the form of a cross *pattée* – one with arms broadening toward the end. Full knights sported the symbol on a white robe, while sergeants – lower-ranking warriors drawn from less aristocratic families – bore it on a black tunic. This apparel had to be worn at all times; no knight could appear in public, even to sit down for a meal, unless properly attired. Templars who fled the field of battle were ceremonially stripped of their robe, much as disgraced soldiers in later times had their badges of rank clipped off them.

THE TEMPLAR SEAL

Showing two knights sharing a single horse, the Templar seal sought to emphasize the order's poverty in its early days. However, the image was never accurate; full knights were in fact allowed three horses each, and as Templar wealth accumulated in later centuries, the claim to poverty came to seem ironic.

The two knight-riders bear shields marked with Templar crosses (1). The inscription (2) reads "Seal of the Soldiers of Christ".

Order of Christ cross

This is the emblem of the historical Order of Christ, founded in Portugal in 1318. It has since become a generic Portuguese emblem, used on the sails of the Portuguese carracks during the Discoveries, by the Portuguese Air Force and on the flag of the Autonomous Region of Madeira. It was also the symbol of the Movimento Nacional-Sindicalista, a fascist group of the early 1930s.

Baphomet

One of the most serious charges brought against the Templars at their trials in France was that they worshipped an idol named Baphomet, thought to be a corruption of the name "Muhammad" (French Mahomet). The accusations no doubt sprang from the suspicion that in the course of their long sojourn in the Muslim lands the Templars' faith had incorporated some elements of Islam. Six hundred years later the French occultist Eliphas Levi borrowed the name and applied it to the goat-headed god that presided over witches' sabbats.

Hospitaller cross

The cross worn by the Hospitallers had arms that each ended in two points, giving their tips the form of indented "v"s. The design seems to have evolved gradually; there is some evidence that initially the knights adopted the patriarchal cross, with twin crosspieces one above the other. Following the move to Malta the insignia developed into the familiar Maltese cross form, with four inward-pointing arrowheads meeting at a central point (see page 12).

ALCHEMY

The scientific quest for spiritual perfection

THREE PRIMES
According to
Paracelsus, the
Three Primes
or Tria Prima
were (from
top to bottom,
above) sulphur
(omnipresent
spirit of life),
mercury (fluid
connection
between the
High and the
Low), and salt
(base matter).

Alchemy is most often thought of now as the ancestor of chemistry, but in its heyday it had much in common with astrology. Both were concerned with the relationship between humankind and the Cosmos. While astrology concentrated on the heavens, alchemy sought correspondences between human nature and the terrestrial world. The two quests were linked through a saying attributed to Hermes Trismegistus, legendary founder of the art: "That which is above is like that which is below; and that which is below like that which is above".

There were alchemists in India, the Arab lands, and in China, where Taoist sages used alchemical techniques to search for the Elixir of Life. In the West the emphasis was on finding a means of transmuting base metals into gold by complex processes of distillation and sublimation and the use of an elusive extra ingredient that came to be known as the Philosopher's Stone. For true seekers, however, the search for gold was always a metaphor for spiritual transformation. What truly interested them was the process itself, for by the doctrine of like for like the embellishment of base metal was seen as a template for an even greater task: the quest for spiritual perfection.

Three Primes

The 16th-century alchemist Paracelsus, a father of modern medicine, defined salt, mercury and sulphur as the Three Primes. Salt (represented by a barred circle) was the type of base matter. Sulphur stood for spirit, and its symbol was an upward-pointing triangle resting on a cross. Mercury, shown as a horned circle set on a cross, was the transmutational agent, serving as the link between the terrestrial and the spiritual.

Philosopher's Stone

A relatively late development in alchemy, the Stone of Knowledge or the Philosopher's Stone (symbol, right) was the name given to the missing ingredient needed to transmute base metals into gold. It seems to have originally taken the form of a tincture or powder rather than an actual stone. Various substances, including sal ammoniac and, later, hydrochloric and sulphuric acid, seemed at different times to hold out promise, never quite fulfilled. Some alchemists claimed to have

THE SEVEN PLANETARY METALS

Alchemists believed that the materials they worked with were microcosmic reflections of the Cosmos as a whole. Thus, each major metal was linked with one of the seven heavenly bodies known to the ancients as planets. These included the Sun and Moon as well as Mercury, Venus, Mars, Jupiter and Saturn. The planets were said to dominate or rule the metals, much as in astrology their conjunctions ruled human destiny. The metals and their associated planets each shared a common symbol (right).

 SOL RULES GOLD

 MERCURIUS RULES QUICKSILVER

 VENUS RULES COPPER

 LUNA RULES SILVER

 MARS RULES IRON

 JUPITER RULES TIN

 SATURNUS RULES LEAD

THE ALCHEMICAL FURNACE

Heat was one of the main instruments for effecting the transmutations that lay at the heart of alchemy. To achieve their calcinations, distillations and sublimations, practitioners needed furnaces. The most important of these was the *athanor*, which took its name from an Arabic transliteration of the Hebrew *tannur* or oven. The *athanor* was designed to be self-feeding, thereby preserving a uniform internal temperature. Typically, the material to be heated was placed in a sealed container within the *athanor* and covered with hot ashes. The process was lengthy, winning the furnace the nickname of *Piger Henricus*, "Lazy Henry".

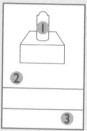

An *athanor* containing the mercury of the philosophers (1), symbolized by the snake. Below, the hermitic bestiary includes a lion (2), representing sulphur, and a phoenix (3), for the Philosopher's Stone, born of the fire of transmutation.

found the stone, among them the French scrivener Nicolas Flamel, who purportedly completed the Great Work in 1382.

Venus and Mars

The conventional symbols used today to indicate gender started life as alchemical signs for what were known as the seven planetary metals (see page 139). The female sign of a cross beneath a circle was associated with copper and the planet Venus; the male sign of an arrow rising from a circle represented iron and Mars.

Four Elements

The four base elements identified by the alchemists were all represented by triangular symbols. A plain triangle pointing upwards stood for fire, while one with a crossbar just below its apex was air; a plain inverted triangle symbolized water, and the same figure crossed was the sign for earth.

Serpent Cross

Part of alchemy's mission was therapeutic, specifically seeking to restore youth and prolong life. Chinese Taoist alchemy was almost exclusively concerned with the quest for the Elixir of Life. In the West alchemists borrowed the traditional medical symbol of the *caduceus* (see pages 86–88) to symbolize this part of their work, but gave it a Christian form by showing the serpent wound around a cross. This serpent cross, sometimes known as Nicolas Flamel's *caduceus*, also had a more specific meaning as a symbol of "fixing the volatile", which involved passing mercury over mineral salts to create a solid.

ROSICRUCIANISM AND HERMETICISM

The mystic path of the rosy cross

The Brethren of the Rose Cross are thought to have originated in Germany early in the 17th century, although enthusiasts have made various attempts to trace their origins further back to remote antiquity. Initially a fraternity devoted to the quest for wisdom and an ascetic lifestyle, and inspired by the tradition of the legendary founder of alchemy Hermes Trismegistus, the Rosicrucians were distinguished from the start by their secrecy; all recruitment was done privately by existing members, and no one outside the movement could know who belonged to it. Initiates claimed knowledge of the alchemical transmutation of base metals into gold, although they set little store by it, concentrating instead on spiritual transformation. Borrowing the language of the Scientific Revolution then getting under way, they spoke of working for the universal reformation of humankind. Subsequent hermetic groups such as the Theosophists and the Order of the Golden Dawn shared their penchant for privacy and the sharing of esoteric knowledge, combining it with a theatricality expressed in exotic costumes and complex rituals.

Flaming sword

This motif owes its significance in both Rosicrucianism and Freemasonry to a reference in the Book of Genesis. When God expelled Adam from the Garden of Eden, he set a "flaming sword, which turned every way" to guard the way to the Tree of Knowledge (see page 144). The sword (sometimes depicted as a weapon with a twisted blade) thus

LUTHER'S SEAL
Martin Luther's seal reflects his theology. The cross in the heart is a reminder that faith in the crucified Christ saves us. The heart in a white rose – colour of the spirits – shows that faith gives joy, comfort and peace.

MELDING MAGIC AND MEDICINE

Rosicrucianism initially made much of its therapeutic mission – one of six requirements of early initiates was to provide medical services free of charge. The *Fama Fraternitatis* describes how the movement's founder, Christian Rosenkreutz, showed natural healing ability, which he refined by lengthy studies in the Arab world – at the time a leader in the sciences. Much of the knowledge he gained on his travels was in fact of alchemy, still considered at the time a legitimate field of study, as indicated by the many works on alchemy then in print, such as Johann Mylius's *Opus medico-chymicum* (1618, below). The original Brotherhood of the Rose Cross thus based its intellectual appeal on a mixture of good works, Christian mysticism and knowledge of the transmutational powers of the alchemists. Its allure was so strong that it spread across Europe.

Hermes Trismegistus (1) and Hippocrates (2) – magic and medicine – support an alchemical seal (3) beneath the Sun and the signs of the zodiac (4), stars (5), minerals (6), microcosm (7) and elements (8).

THE TREE OF KNOWLEDGE

Rosicrucians and most later hermetic groups worked mainly within the Christian tradition, but also looked outside it to the Arab world (science) and Judaism (Kabbalah). The Theosophists drew on Buddhism and Hinduism. Later adepts were aware of the Gnostics, particularly their heterodox reading of the Garden of Eden story, in which the serpent became the hero. By urging Eve to taste the apple, it was encouraging humankind to overcome its God-given limitations and itself become like the gods. For the Gnostics, the route to such power lay through knowledge, the forbidden fruit of the tree – a theme illustrated in books such as the 18th-century German *Secret Symbols of the Rosicrucians* (below).

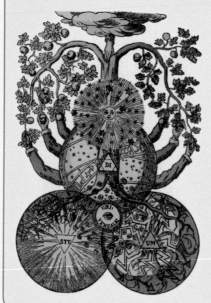

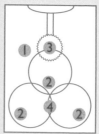

Hands (1) reach out to pluck the fruits of the Tree of Knowledge, rooted in the three worlds (2) of God's creation. A solar symbol (3) radiates light on the scene; below it is the lesser sun of spiritual illumination (4).

represented the final marker on the way toward the tree and also the last obstacle to be overcome in reaching it.

Rose cross

Associated particularly with the cult of the Virgin Mary, the rose was a Christian symbol long before the Rosicrucians appropriated it for their rose cross (right). A cross within a rose was the seal of the German reformer Martin Luther (see page 142), leading some scholars to speculate that the original brotherhood had a Protestant agenda: certainly the movement's earliest text, the *Fama Fraternitatis*, has the supposed founder Christian Rosenkreutz born in Wartburg Castle, where Luther himself took refuge.

Rayed cross

A symbol of the Order of the Golden Dawn, this emblem features a cross perched on the apex of a pyramid containing a stylized image of the Sun rising from the sea. Drawing on both Christian and ancient Egyptian imagery, the design encapsulates the eclectic mix of influences that went into this influential group, which included the eminent Irish poet W.B. Yeats among its members.

Portal

This is the name given by many hermetic groups to the points of access to esoteric knowledge and to paths of initiation into secret orders. The Portal Grade was also the name of an initiation rite undertaken by would-be adepts of the Order of the Golden Dawn.

FREEMASONRY

Disciples of the divine architect

Freemasons belong to a fraternal organization that is arguably the best-subscribed of all esoteric societies. Its symbolism accords a particular place of honour to the biblical Temple of King Solomon, held to be the perfect edifice, having been built under divine guidance. Masons even trace their name back to the craftsmen who built the Temple, viewing them as a uniquely inspired brotherhood bound by oaths of confidentiality to protect their trade and its secrets. Other

Traditionally, Freemasonry has passed on its teachings with the aid of tracing boards, a term chosen to recall the design-inscribed boards believed to have been used by ancient stonemasons to cut stone to size. The boards are colourful devices that depict selected symbols thought suitable for revelation to members at different stages of their initiation.

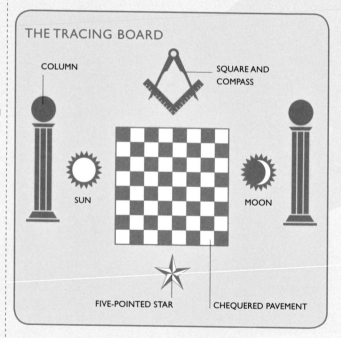

THE TRACING BOARD

COLUMN

SQUARE AND COMPASS

SUN

MOON

FIVE-POINTED STAR

CHEQUERED PAVEMENT

members have sought over the years to trace an alternative, non-Judeo-Christian lineage, seeking roots instead in ancient Egyptian, Pythagorean or hermeneutical traditions. On current evidence, however, it seems likely that the movement dates no further back than early modern Europe, with the first clearly identified groups operating in Britain in the 17th century.

Freemasonry attained a peak in the Enlightenment era. The Grand Lodge of England was founded in 1717, and the three degrees of Masonic membership – Apprentice, Fellow, Master Mason – were established by that time. The tripartite arrangement was symbolized in the triangle, a shape adopted by Sir John Soane for his Freemasons' Hall in London, sadly now demolished. Freemasons also became influential in continental Europe and the USA, where many of the political architects of the young republic were initiates, among them George Washington himself.

Apron
The first gift bestowed on a newly initiated apprentice, the apron is an emblem of purity in life and conduct, and – like the tracing board (opposite) – a reference to Masonic conceptions of the ancient stonemason's craft. The earliest Masons inherited the three degrees of membership from the structure of the medieval craft guild whose name they inherited.

Chequered pavement
Claimed to be modelled on the mosaic pavement in Solomon's Temple itself, the chequered pavement represents the vicissitudes of life and the pairing of opposites (such as Sun and Moon). Specifically, it refers to the coexistence of good and evil in the human world.

EYE OF PROVIDENCE
The reverse of the Great Seal of the United States shows an all-seeing Eye of Providence atop a pyramid of 13 layers, one for each of the original states. The eye is a Masonic symbol, and there was at least one Mason – Benjamin Franklin – on the committee that approved the design, although he is not thought to have been directly responsible for its inclusion.

Compass

The compass and the square together embody ancient craft masonry and a correctly lived life. The compass suggests the role of the rational mind in ordering conduct and circumscribing desire.

Square

An emblem of order, the square implies conscious purpose and control over the emotions. Masons meet "on the square", a phrase that implies acting honourably.

Beehive

The beehive symbolizes the Masons' commitment to hard work and to contributing to society. It conveys the idea of the Masonic brotherhood as a creative community working for a common purpose.

Scales

Among Freemasonry's many borrowed emblems are the scales, standing for balance and measure. This symbol can be traced back to Roman statues of Justitia, the Roman personification of justice, who carried a pair of scales to weigh the merits of each case and a sword to punish wrongdoing.

Skull and crossbones

Famed as a symbol of ocean-going pirates, the skull and crossbones actually dates further back in time as an image of physical decay and death opening the way to spiritual rebirth. This is its meaning in some Masonic traditions, though non-initiates have generally seen such imagery as confirmation of the supposedly bloodthirsty nature of some Masonic vows.

THE SEAL OF MISRAIM

One pseudo-historical tradition seeks to trace Freemasonry's origins back to ancient Egypt. The so-called Egyptian Rite owed much of its initial success to the 18th-century adventurer – and Mason – Count Cagliostro, who established an Egyptian lodge in Paris. The idea spread, surviving the Count's own disappearance (he is thought to have died in an Italian prison) and was later championed by the Italian patriot Guiseppe Garibaldi. It is still internationally active today.

A French seal of Misraim (an early name for the Egyptian Rite) features a host of Masonic symbols including an Orphic egg (1) (see page 86), scales (2), a pair of compasses (3), an Eye of Providence (4) (see page 10), and a flight of steps representing the path to illumination (5).

WICCA AND NEO-PAGANISM
Folk cults for the modern world

SHIELD KNOT
In its ancient Norse form the four-cornered knot combines a swastika (see page 152) and a solar cross motif – but the basic form is much older and can be found in Mesopotamia. In both places its purpose was protective, invoking the four corners of the Earth – a meaning echoed in modern usage.

Wicca is the modern form of witchcraft, most famously championed by the English author and folklorist Gerald Gardner in the mid-20th century, who expanded upon the earlier work of Margaret Murray (see page 153). Wicca claims to trace its origins to an ancient underground set of beliefs sometimes referred to as the "old religion". This in turn taps into surviving remnants of pre-Christian paganism. Unlike most other religions and cults, Wicca does not have a standardized canon, but common features include the worship of a God and Goddess, often symbolized as the Sun and the Moon, which embody the counterbalancing forces found throughout nature.

The word "pagan", deriving from the Latin *paganus* or "rustic", was initially a pejorative term applied by Christians to the polytheistic folk religions that their own monotheistic faith supplanted. From the 4th century CE on, paganism was outlawed and persecuted. In later centuries symbols such as the Wiccan pentacle – a five-pointed star in a circle (see page 153) – became clandestine signs by which initiates could recognize one another.

Triskelion

Interlocking swirling triple spirals adorn the entrance stone of the Neolithic site of Newgrange in Ireland, while related forms of the pattern were incorporated into the designs of brooches (right) by the Germanic Anglo-Saxon tribes.

The so-called triskelion design (see also page 18) is in fact found throughout the world, with many cultural variants and meanings.

THE CROSS AND SWASTIKA

A Hiberno-Saxon figure used to decorate the handle of a bucket.

Symmetry and repetition typify Bronze Age European artistry. This bronze figure (left) bears on his chest a cross (1) within a square (2), creating four boxes each containing a stylized swastika (3), thought to represent awe-inspiring elemental power in the form of lightning.

Modern Celtic-inspired Wiccans use the triskelion sign to represent the idea of the triple goddess, who is part maiden, part mother and part crone. Other modifications of the design form the three-legged flag motifs of the Isle of Man and of Sicily, while on the opposite side of the world, the Korean *sam-taeguk* – three interlocking commas of contrasting primary colours organized within a circle – is an Oriental variant that also echoes the *yin-yang* motif. Some people have claimed that the ancient Celts' fascination with triplication may have its roots in their idea of the elemental and the three realms of material existence: land, sea and sky.

SWASTIKA
A curved
swastika was
the emblem
of the Thule
Society, an
early 20th-
century occult
order founded
in southern
Germany. The
organization's
nationalist
agenda is
believed to
have influenced
Nazism.
The curved
swastika
symbol was
later adopted
by the SS
Nordland
division in
World War II.

Swastika

Most readily recognized now as an icon of 20th-century Nazism, the swastika in fact has a venerable history. It was found not only in Bronze and Iron Age Europe but also featured prominently in ancient Asia's dharmic religions (see pages 104–105). The name itself derives from the Sanskrit *svástika*, denoting "well being". The motif is normally taken to represent a "sun cross" with arms bent to lend a sense of momentum and movement.

THE POWER OF RUNES

Divination with runes – the script used by Germanic and Scandinavian peoples – is a modern form of pagan-inspired augury. In *De Germania*, Tacitus described how people in the north German lands used to mark twigs and throw them to tell omens. New Age gurus have devised systems by which tokens marked with runes are cast to foretell events, in the manner of *I Ching* or Tarot card readings.

An 11th-century Viking memorial stone using a popular carved snake design, which indicates how the runic inscription should be read – along the snake's body from the head to the tail. It was erected in Gripsholm, Sweden, by a mother grieving for her sons Harald and Ingvars, whom she praises for having "fed the eagle" (killed many in battle).

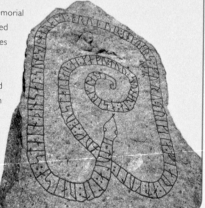

Horned God

The concept of the Horned God owes much to the British anthropologist Margaret Murray, whose 1921 work *The Witch Cult in Western Europe* was a key text in the development of the modern Wiccan tradition. Murray argued that medieval witches were the inheritors of an ancient underground religious tradition stretching back to prehistoric times, whose central focus was a horned male deity (left, here in the form of Pan, the Greek goat-god). The Celts venerated this divinity as Cernunnos, Lord of the Animals, associated with fertility and hunting. Murray's theories have since been criticized by scholars who have questioned her use of sources. Under feminist influence, many Wiccan groups have supplanted the Horned God with a Mother Goddess figure, often depicted as a triple goddess in the form of three lunar phases.

Pentacle

Often treated as synonymous with the pentagram (see pages 13–14), which has long been renowned as a magical symbol, the word "pentacle" is also used in Wiccan circles to refer to talismans of paper, parchment or metal used in magical invocations. Sometimes these feature protective symbols that may include pentagrams, although hexagrams and magic squares are equally likely to appear. The pentagram itself, inscribed within a circle, is now accepted by the US Department of Veterans' Affairs as a headstone marker for Wiccan graves in military cemeteries.

FURTHER READING

DICTIONARIES OF SYMBOLS AND OTHER GENERAL WORKS

1001 Symbols, by Jack Tresidder *(Duncan Baird Publishers, 2003)*

Brewer's Dictionary of Phrase and Fable *(Wordsworth Editions, 1993)*

Cassell Dictionary of Superstitions, by David Pickering *(Brockhampton Press, 1998)*

The Complete Dictionary of Symbols in Myth, Art and Literature, ed. by Jack Tresidder *(Duncan Baird Publishers, 2004)*

The Continuum Encyclopedia of Symbols, by Udo Becker *(Continuum, 2000)*

Dictionary of Subjects and Symbols in Art, by James Hall *(John Murray, 1989)*

A Dictionary of Symbols, by J.E. Cirlot, *(Dover, 2002)*

Dictionary of Symbols in Art, by Sarah Carr-Gomm *(Duncan Baird Publishers, 2000)*

Funk & Wagnall's Standard Dictionary of Folklore, Mythology, and Legend, ed. by Maria Leach and Jerome Fried *(Harper San Francisco, 1984)*

The Golden Bough, by Sir James Fraser *(Wordsworth Editions, reissued 1993)*

An Illustrated Encyclopedia of Traditional Symbols, by J.C. Cooper *(Thames & Hudson, 1979)*

Images and Symbols, by Mircea Eliade and Philip Mairet *(Princeton University Press, 1991)*

Man and his Symbols, by Carl Gustav Jung *(Laurel Press, reissued 1997)*

The Myth of the Eternal Return, by Mircea Eliade *(Princeton University Press, reissued 2005)*

Nature and its Symbols, by Lucia Impelluso *(Getty Publishing, 2005)*

The Penguin Dictionary of Symbols, by Jean Chevalier and Alain Gheerbrant, *(Penguin Reference, 1996)*

The Secret Language of Symbols, by David Fontana *(Duncan Baird Publishers, 2001)*

Symbols and Allegories in Art, by Matilde Battistini *(Getty Publishing, 2005)*

Symbols – Encyclopedia of Western Signs and Ideograms, by Carl G. Liungman *(HME Publishing, 2004)*

Symbols, Signs and Visual Codes, by Mark O'Connor and Raje Airey *(Southwater, 2007)*

GUIDES TO SYMBOLISM IN INDIVIDUAL TRADITIONS

African Symbols, by Heike Owusu *(Sterling, 2007)*

Chinese Symbolism and Art Motifs, by C.A.S. Williams *(Tuttle Publishing, 2006)*

Codex Magica: Secret Signs, Mysterious Symbols, and Hidden Codes of the Illuminati, by Texe Marrs *(RiverCrest Publishing, 2005)*

A Dictionary of Chinese Symbols, by Wolfram Eberhard *(Routledge, 1988)*

The Encyclopedia of Jewish Symbols, by Ellen Frankel and Betsy Platkin Teutsch *(Jason Aronson, 1996)*

The Encyclopedia of Tibetan Symbols and Motifs, by Robert Beer *(Shambhala, 1999)*

Gods, Demons and Symbols of Ancient Mesopotamia, by Jeremy Black, Anthony Green and Tessa Rickards *(British Museum Press, 1992)*

An Illustrated Dictionary of the Gods and Symbols of Ancient Mexico and the Maya, by Mary Miller and Karl Taube *(Thames & Hudson, 1997)*

Masonic and Occult Symbols Illustrated, by Cathy Burns *(Sharing, 1998)*

Myths and Symbols in Indian Art and Civilization, by Heinrich Zimmer *(Princeton University Press, 1992)*

Signs, Symbols and Omens: An Illustrated Guide to Magical and Spiritual Symbolism, by Raymond Buckland *(Llewellyn Publications, 2003)*

Symbol and Magic in Egyptian Art, by Richard H. Wilkinson *(Thames & Hudson, 1999)*

Symbols of Native America, by Heike Owusu *(Sterling, 1999)*

INDEX

ACKNOWLEDGMENTS

Picture Credits

The publisher would like to thank the following people, museums and photographic libraries for permission to reproduce their material. Every care has been taken to trace copyright holders. However, if we have omitted anyone we apologize and will, if informed, make corrections in any future edition.

Abbreviations:
BAL   Bridgeman Art Library
WFA   Werner Forman Archive

Page 1 © The Trustees of the British Museum; **81** Egyptian National Museum, Cairo/BAL; **85** Robert Harding Picture Library/Photolibrary; **87** © The Trustees of the British Museum; **91** © The Trustees of the British Museum; **93** Victoria & Albert Museum; **97** Victoria & Albert Museum; **99** © The Trustees of the British Museum; **103** © The Trustees of the British Museum; **107** Corbis Sygma/Desai Noshir; **110** The Wellcome Collection/Michael Holford; **113** BAL/Private Collection; **115** Archivo Iconográfico, S.A./Corbis; **116** Courtesy of The Jewish Museum, London; **118** Alinari Archives; **121** Edifice; **122** © The Trustees of the British Museum; **125** Musée du Louvre/Art Archive/Gianni Dagli Orti; **126** WFA/Private Collection; **129** © Baha'i International Community; **131** Alinari Archives; **135 top** Corbis/Sandro Vannini; **135 bottom** John Heseltine; **136** Corbis Sygma/Origlia Franco; **144** AKG-Images; **149** Musée du Grand Orient/Art Archive/Marc Charmet; **151** Viking Ship Museum, Bygdoy/WFA; **152** Corbis/Kevin Schafer